Help Lord!
I'm Trying
to Relate

Help Lord! I'm Trying to Relate

Lessons on effective relationships from the book of Genesis

Katey Moreland

Sovereign World

Sovereign World Ltd
PO Box 777
Tonbridge
Kent TN11 0ZS
England

Copyright © 2004 Katey Moreland

All rights reserved. No part of this publication may be reproduced, stored in a retrieval system, or transmitted in any form or by any means, electronic, mechanical, photocopying or otherwise, without the prior written consent of the publisher. Short extracts may be used for review purposes.

All Scripture quotations are taken from the Spirit-Filled Life Bible unless otherwise stated. Copyright © 1991 by Thomas Nelson Publishers Inc. Nashville, USA

Scripture quotations taken from the Amplified Bible are Copyright © 1954, 1958, 1962, 1964, 1965, 1987 by The Lockman Foundation

Scripture quotations taken from the New English Bible are Copyright © 1970 by Oxford and Cambridge Universities Presses

ISBN 1 85240 386 1

The publishers aim to produce books which will help to extend and build up the Kingdom of God. We do not necessarily agree with every view expressed by the author, or with every interpretation of Scripture expressed. We expect each reader to make his/her judgment in the light of their own understanding of God's Word and in an attitude of Christian love and fellowship.

Cover design by CCD, www.ccdgroup.co.uk
Typeset by CRB Associates, Reepham, Norfolk
Printed by Clays, St Ives plc

Dedication

*A gift for Marg,
a precious friend the Lord asked me
to share this study with.
May she, like you,
be blessed in the reading of it.*

*With a grateful heart towards my Daddy,
Father God, whose comforts delight my soul
(Psalm 94:19).*

Contents

	Acknowledgments	9
Chapter 1	Mirror Image: God and Mankind	11
Chapter 2	Perfect Match: Adam and Eve	15
Chapter 3	Brother's Keeper: Cain and Abel	26
Chapter 4	Family Traits: Seth and Enoch vs. Cain and Lamech	31
Chapter 5	Float On! Noah and the Lord	34
Chapter 6	World Leaders: Noah's Sons	42
Chapter 7	Friend and Confidant: Abraham and the Lord	46
Chapter 8	It's a Promise! Abraham and Sarah	69
Chapter 9	Family Connections: Lot and the Lord	77
Chapter 10	The Quiet Man: Isaac and the Lord	81
Chapter 11	Meant to Be: Isaac and Rebekah	89
Chapter 12	Building Trust: Jacob and the Lord	95
Chapter 13	Lost and Found: Jacob and Esau	111
Chapter 14	Love Triangle: Jacob, Rachel and Leah	117
Chapter 15	Meet the Tribes: Jacob and Sons	123
Chapter 16	Love Conquers All: Joseph and the Lord	134
Chapter 17	Love and Hate: Joseph and His Brothers	147
	Bibliography	158
	Helpful Addresses	159

Acknowledgments

Thanks to friends and family for their support, especially those who willingly became living examples in my writing, and to Ruth Hawkey for directing me to God's choice of publisher.

My special thanks go to my sister, Norah, who always gave me the space to be creative by willingly taking over caring for our mother. Without her support my study would undoubtedly still be 'in progress'.

Chapter 1
Mirror Image: God and Mankind

> *'In the beginning was the Word, and the Word was with God, and the Word was God. He was in the beginning with God. All things were made through Him, and without Him nothing was made that was made.'* (John 1:1–3)

When God had created the heavens and the earth, and filled them with good things, He said,

> *'Let Us make man in Our image; let them have dominion over ... all the earth.'* (Genesis 1:26)

God was pleased with all of His creation, and yet even before man was created we can see that he was to be considered more special than all other creations; man was to be made in the image of God and was to be given the privilege and responsibility of ruling over the earth. At the end of every day, God looked at His work and agreed that *'it was good'*. There was an excitement brimming forth from God, as on the sixth day, the day that man was created, *'God saw everything that He had made, and indeed it was very good'* (Genesis 1:31). God was in love with man and so man made the picture complete.

> *'So God created man in His own image; in the image of God He created him; male and female He created them.'*
> (Genesis 1:27)

Directly from this scripture we learn that we humans, not just the male population, are created in God's image and likeness. Male and female have equal status in God's eyes. This sense of equality for man and woman is further substantiated in the account of the creation of Eve. God says she is comparable to Adam (Genesis 2:18) and that they are so evenly matched that the two can be compared, whereas no one can be compared to God.

We can never be compared to God; not one of us can ever be a match for Him who is all-powerful, all-mighty and all-wonderful God. Yet, we are made in His image and are therefore called to be a reflection of God. A reflection is made of light bouncing off an object. It does not depend on the object itself, but on the positioning of the light upon the object. Christ is the light and we are the 'object' of His attention. We are created in God's image and therefore have the potential to be like Him. Satan would have us believe that it is impossible to be like God, and would drag us into a sense of failure and/or hopelessness; anything to stop us from living in the blessings of our Heavenly Father. However, the Lord would say to us *'Therefore you shall be perfect, just as your Father in heaven is perfect'* (Matthew 5:48). This is not 'be perfect in your own strength' for such an act is impossible. Rather it means, 'become whole as I am whole'. The only way to become whole is to remember that we are not expected to be God's equal, but His reflection. As we allow the light of Christ to shine upon us, healing our pains, revealing our deceptions, and loving our characters, then we are free to become the people that He created us to be and therefore, reflect His glorious image. It's an ongoing process; none of us have made it, but many of us are on the journey! If you've never known Father God's love in a personal way, invite Him into your life and He will respond genuinely and directly to you.

Despite being a Christian for ten years, I knew nothing of the love of the Father until I forgave my earthly father for the damage that he had caused my family. Since that time, I have had many precious moments in the presence of my Heavenly Father – the most intimate and fulfilling time being at a 'Creativity and Healing' course with Ellel Ministries. The purpose of the course was for participants to find and enjoy their inner-creativity; not all are artistic, but all are creative, as we are born in the image of the Creator. Many activities were available from sewing, to card making, to 'fun in the messy area'. I chose the latter option, remaining there for the whole of the course. Others came and went, but in my spirit, I was completely alone with Father God! I began by splashing paint onto a five feet long piece of paper, using colour to represent my feelings. When I used red to represent my pain, I was hardly able to stop! Gold and silver, God's grace and mercy, flooded the picture to cover my shame and pain. I poured a rainbow of colours into a bowl to make a 'footprint' border – in receiving healing, life was beginning to appear vibrant. A classmate needed to support me as I set my footprints upon the paper, indicating how we need to support one another in our walk with God. To complete my nursery-style 'masterpiece' I wrote, 'My Daddy accepts me as I am' (the first time I truly believed this). I wrote the letters without any consideration for colour sequence or spacing; perfection was not important, it was only having quality time with my Daddy that mattered. It was truly an awesome time, with Father God taking me back to my childhood to give me all the nurturing love I had not received from my earthly father. And although I have been blessed to receive much ministry into my life, counselling could not bring the depth of healing that Father God brought into that very personal time with Him. After that course, I was so much more whole than I was before, and unlike usual ministry, it didn't hurt!

Personal application

Father God was pleased to create man in His image, making us with gifts of creativity and freedom in order to relate to Him. If our self-image has been damaged we may not feel worthy to be in God's presence, or cannot believe He enjoys our company. We are called to be a beautiful reflection of Christ, but may instead feel more like a broken old mirror. If something is broken, then who is the best person to restore it than the one who made it? So too, the best place for us to take our brokenness is to the Creator, allowing ourselves to be with God and receive His love and restoration directly into our spirits. The following prayer may help:

> *Lord God,*
> *I accept that I am made in Your image and likeness* [Genesis 1:26], *acknowledging that You have formed my inward parts; You have covered me in my mother's womb. I choose to praise You because I am wonderfully made* [Psalm 139:14].
>   *As a reflection of Christ, I choose to allow Your light to shine upon me, to reveal to me all that You find pleasant about me. I ask for the revelation that I am the apple of Your eye to penetrate*

> *deeply into my Spirit, bringing healing and wholeness* [Psalm 17:8]. *I also give You permission to shine Your light upon all that is not a part of Your will for my life – sin that brings ugliness and filth in to my life, as well as pain that I have buried and find difficult to let go.*
>
> *I pray by Your grace that I may be able to deal with the issues You bring up, releasing them completely to You. I choose to leave each issue at the foot of the cross and begin my life anew with You. I desire to be the reflection that You have called me to be, and declare afresh that I allow You to be Lord of every area of my life. Amen!*

This prayer may be the beginning of healing, or it may bring a mighty revelation to you of who you are in God's eyes. A wonderful psalm to meditate on is Psalm 139. Read it slowly and carefully, allowing the Holy Spirit to reveal to you how very beautiful you are in God's sight. When you know you are loved, accepted and understood by God, it is so much easier to enjoy life to the full. Consider creative ways of spending time with God. We don't need to kneel in prayer to be in communion with our Lord. You can take a walk together, write poetry, bang a drum, or draw a picture; there are no limits. For those interested in taking part in a 'Creativity and Healing' course with Ellel Ministries, details can be found in the 'Helpful Addresses' section.

Chapter 2
Perfect Match: Adam and Eve

God created Adam in His own image, placed him in the beautiful Garden of Eden, gave him authority over everything and often visited with him (Genesis 3:8). Yet God, seeing a need not yet fulfilled in Adam's life, announced,

> '... It is not good that man should be alone; I will make him a helper comparable to him.' (Genesis 2:18)

Collin's Thesaurus[1] gives the following synonyms for the adjective 'comparable'; *on a par, a match for, as good as, equal, in a class with*. Take time to slot these synonyms in and you will begin to see God's plan for male/female relationships. God created Eve from one of Adam's ribs. Adam responded, *'This is now bone of my bones and flesh of my flesh'* (Genesis 2:23), emphasising God's plan that intimacy was to be an important part of godly male/female relationships. For this reason a man and wife shall become one flesh. In Adam and Eve's case, husband and wife were, quite literally, one flesh!

> 'And they were both naked ... and were not ashamed.' (Genesis 2:25)

They did not yet know sin and therefore, shame could have no hold over them. In a sinful world, we relate negatively to cover up our own sense of inadequacy. With a desire to return to God's plan for honest and shameless communication, one couple I know go out on a monthly 'date', leaving all distractions behind, to bear their soul to one another. Unfortunately, Adam and Eve

---

[1] *Collins Gem English Thesaurus* (third edition, reprint 2001).

did not remain in shameless communion for long. The serpent soon beguiled them, persuading Eve to go against the commandment of God. Together they chose to sin.

The account of man's first sin contains many clues for us in how to deal with temptation. Satan, the god of this world, was thrown out of heaven after attempting to supersede God's authority (Isaiah 14:14; Luke 10:18). Unable to taint God's character, Satan attempts to destroy God's plan by tempting God's reflection, man, to sin against God. Satan, we are told, is subtle and not at all direct, suggesting to Eve that she should question God's word and His intended meaning. In our lives, Satan continues to tempt us in the same way. Questioning is not wrong, but answering without knowledge is dangerous; Solomon articulates, *'Where there is no revelation, the people cast off restraint'* (Proverbs 29:18). According to the Word of God, Christians who commit adultery lack knowledge and do not know that they are destroying their own souls (Proverbs 6:32). Jesus once answered the Pharisees, *'Are you not therefore mistaken, because you do not know the Scriptures nor the power of God?'* (Mark 12:24). How else can church leaders condone homosexual relationships and tell us that signs and wonders were only for 'Bible times'?

Satan, I believe, chose to tempt Eve because she had not received the commandment directly from God but from Adam, whom God had directed before Eve was even created (Genesis 2:17). We must teach one another; yet receiving God's word, commandment or promise holds a greater power and authority when received into our spirits directly from God. When we hear the preacher sharing 'powerful truths', it's our responsibility to transport the knowledge from our minds to our spirits in order to produce lasting fruits. Meditating on God's word is the only way to do this, allowing the Holy Spirit to speak the truth to you. If your mind declares that God will protect you from evil, but your spirit is unable to believe this, then Satan will suggest that you put your trust in someone or something else (e.g. lucky charms). Allowing the Holy Spirit to declare God's faithfulness directly into your spirit sets you free to trust God, denying Satan the power to confuse you. Satan cannot make any of us sin; the choice is always ours. However, as with Eve, he will tempt us to question God's authority and intent so that we choose to sin. Having enticed Eve into discussion, Satan was able to argue against God's honourable character. The lesson here is *never get into discussion with Satan!* When Satan was allowed to tempt Jesus, our Lord never entered into discussion, but rather responded to each question with the Word of God (Luke 4:1–13). When God's Word has the last say, Satan is made powerless and will flee from you (James 4:7).

Satan, the father of lies, suggested to Eve that God had not spoken the truth:

> '... *You will not surely die. For God knows that in the day you eat of it* [the tree of knowledge] *your eyes will be opened, and you will be like God, knowing good and evil.*' (Genesis 3:4–5)

Eve had previously lived contentedly in the Garden of Eden, aware but uninterested in the tree. Satan gave her a reason to look upon that tree. Job knew the power of 'looking' and so made a covenant with his eyes not to look upon that which would make him lust (Job 31:1). *We must also make a covenant with our eyes if we are not to sin.* We may want to excuse ourselves and say 'I'm only looking.' However, on looking, Eve was able to persuade herself to take the fruit, reasoning it was *'pleasant to the eyes'* (Genesis 3:6). Ungodly images cloud our vision. Late night channel flicking is especially dangerous; raunchy movies suggests fornication (sex before marriage) is 'natural' rather than a sin; images glorifying violence suggest a temper is 'cool' rather than cruel, and adultery is presented as a second-chance to find 'real love'. As soon as the eye enjoys looking at that which is sinful, the rest of our flesh wants to become involved, and the mind creates a convincing argument to fulfil the lust of the flesh.

Eve could have walked away from temptation by choosing to refute Satan's lies with the Word of God, making a conscious decision to follow His commands. As it was, she not only ate that which was forbidden, but also shared it with her husband. This again, is an example of the subtlety of Satan. Had Satan gone directly to Adam, Adam would have probably corrected him outright and refused to disobey the command that he had received directly from God. Yet, our principles can be chipped away, without realising the attack, when another human suggests we 'cheat a little'. After all, how likely was it that God would notice that fruit had gone from the Tree of Knowledge? They could have tasted the fruit just the once! 'I won't tell, if you don't!' may have been their agreement. Little did Adam and Eve realise that their behaviour would reveal their sin!

> *'Then the eyes of both of them were opened, and they knew that they were naked; and they sewed fig leaves together and made themselves coverings.'* (Genesis 3:7)

Adam and Eve tried to cover their shame, a trait that we all too easily follow. However, the shame is not removed, it is only hidden, granting it stronger power internally. Shame is heavy on man's soul, weighing us down. We, like Adam and Eve, lose our innocence and exchange it for shame, when sin enters our lives. Adam and Eve remained disgraced, but we can be set free from the shame of sin by accepting the Lord Jesus Christ into our hearts and lives; He took all our shame on the cross. What a wonderful message of salvation! No longer in condemnation, by the grace of God we stand!

Because of their shame, Adam and Eve hid themselves when they heard God walking in the garden. We have inherited their sinful ways; following 'human nature', we hide ourselves from God when we have sinned. It is also human nature to shift blame, rather than take responsibility for one's actions. When God asked Adam, *'Have you eaten from the tree of which I commanded you that you should not eat?'* (Genesis 3:11), Adam took no responsibility for his action. Firstly, he apportioned some of the blame to God, and secondly to Eve, *'The woman whom **You** gave to be with me, she gave me of the tree, and I ate'* (Genesis 3:12). So too, Eve responded, *'The serpent deceived me, and I ate'* (Genesis 3:13). Adam and Eve were created in the image of God and therefore possessed the capacity to respond in a godly way; Adam's rightful authority as husband should have led him to correct his wife, 'No, we shall not eat', whereas Eve needed to recognise that she had chosen to believe Satan's portrayal of God's character, rather than her husband's.

For every sin there must be a punishment. Because of Adam and Eve's sin, the human race was cursed. To the serpent, God pronounced *'enmity between you and the woman, and between your seed and her Seed; He shall bruise your head, and you shall bruise His heel'* (Genesis 3:15). Hostility is bound to be a characteristic of a relationship between the tempter and the tempted. Satan had tricked Eve into believing a lie – a lie that cost her life. If that were the whole story, if man was left in a cycle of endless hostility with Satan and without any promise of salvation, then there would be no hope to sustain life. However, our God devised a plan to save us from Satan's trickery:

> *'But when the fullness of the time had come, God sent forth His Son, born of a woman, born under the law, to redeem those who were under the law ...'* (Galatians 4:4–5)

All things are put under Jesus' feet (Ephesians 1:22); He bruises Satan's head on our behalf. Satan continues to *'make war with the rest of her offspring* [believers], *who keep the commandments of God and have the testimony of Jesus Christ'* (Revelation 12:17). However, in our battles, we are encouraged to *'be wise in what is good, and simple concerning evil. And the God of peace will crush Satan under your feet shortly'* (Romans 16:19–20).

Eve's disobedience resulted in the introduction of 'women's problems'. Pain in childbirth is a direct consequence of sin and is therefore a curse upon a sinful world (Genesis 3:16). Yet, for those who choose to receive Christ into their lives, it is promised,

> *'Christ has redeemed us from the curse of the law, having become a curse for us (for it is written "Cursed is everyone who hangs on a tree").'* (Galatians 3:13)

The blessing that counteracts the curse is like a saving account that a parent has opened on our behalf. Becoming a Christian can be likened to receiving the bankbook. The account is in our name, we have the 'book', but unless we take it to the bank, asking for a withdrawal, we will not receive any of the savings. Christ has taken the curse of not only painful labour, but also all 'women related' problems. Therefore, women can (and should!) claim redemption through Jesus Christ from period pains, premenstrual tension (PMT), pregnancy complications, morning sickness, 'the change' – basically anything that is related to the womb.

During my counselling training with Ellel ministries, a lady asked me to pray with her for God's guidance. Having 'women's problems', she wanted to know if she should continue with medication given to her by her doctor or have a hysterectomy. I shared my belief that neither proposition was God's best for her, and suggested that we should declare the truth that Jesus died on the cross to set her free, carrying the curse for her. At the following ministry evening, she sought me out to tell me God had healed her the very night we prayed. Completely healed, her doctor confirmed that she no longer needed medication or an operation in order to live a normal life. Women who have also had hysterectomy operations can benefit from having the curse broken over their lives in order to feel like 'full women' again. Having heard the above story, another lady, having already had a hysterectomy, asked me to pray with her. I had little understanding of her pain, yet knew a simple truth – if God promises it in His Word, then it is true! So we prayed the curse to be reversed and where there was emptiness that God would fill her anew; where she was robbed of the sense of womanhood, that the Lord would richly endow her. And then we sat quietly as the Lord ministered to her, freeing her from the misconception of self, and filling her with wonder at the beautiful woman that God had created her to be. For God (who is *not* a man in the sky who is insensitive to women's pain), will emancipate all who ask for freedom. It sounds quite incredible, but there is one man who suffered all of women's problems – Jesus Christ, who took the curse upon the tree!

> *'Surely He has borne our griefs*
> *And carried our sorrows ...*
> *The chastisement for our peace was upon Him,*
> *And by His stripes we are healed.'* (Isaiah 53:4, 5)

To woman God also said, *'Your desire shall be for your husband, and he shall rule over you'* (Genesis 3:16). A direct consequence of sin, not God's ordination, is of man ruling over woman and blaming her for their sin and its consequences. She, riddled with guilt over the wedge now between them, desired to appease her husband. Paul, in writing to the Ephesians, compares God's order in marriage to the relationship of Adam and Eve before 'the fall' (Ephesians 5:22–33). From the beginning, God gave authority to Adam; woman being formed from man shows she is a part of him. This is not to claim superiority for the husband; each part of the body has its own important role to play. Authority, also, should not be confused with control! When sin reigns, there is control. A wife is not requested to submit to ungodly control, but to the godly authority of her husband, who in turn is called to love her as he loves his own body (Ephesians 5:28), even sacrificing himself for her as Jesus sacrificed Himself for His bride, the Church (Ephesians 5:25). In the body of Christ, married couples are invited back to the place where Adam and Eve dwelt before they knew sin and shame; they are called to go beyond the system of control and appeasement into the realms of unconditional love and acceptance.

For Adam's part in sinning against God, the ground became cursed. 'Working the ground' would demand sweat and toil, even producing unwanted thorns and thistles (Genesis 3:17–19). The Word of God has an antidote for every curse ever mentioned. I believe the remedy for a life of toil is partaking in the Sabbath rest. In our 24/7 post-modern societies, we are all too busy to take a day off to rest in God. It's actually *hard work* following the Lord's command to rest! Toil is a product of Adam's sin, and the Sabbath is God's sign to us that He cleanses us from our sin (Ezekiel 20:12). Adam worked before the fall, caring for the environment and animals, yet only after the fall did work become a life of toil. For those of us who are hard workers, we tend to think 'finish the work, and then rest.' However, *Sabbath* means 'interruption'; God would have us change our focus to leave other jobs left unfinished and choose to trust our work to Him. My own experience of following the Lord's instruction to rest on the Sabbath is that I'm more energised and focused, achieving a great deal more in six days than I could independently manage in seven. Carers and parents alike may feel they can never have a Sabbath rest, being on duty 24/7. The Lord has shown me that the attitude towards rest is what is important, instructing me to give ungrudgingly in the area of personal needs, while leaving non-urgent tasks alone. This attitude to rest can then reach our spirits on our workdays, enabling us to be more productive, yet amazingly toil-free.

The issue of death was a contentious one in the Garden of Eden. God had warned Adam that if he should eat of the tree of knowledge *'in the day that you eat of it you shall surely die'* (Genesis 2:17). The serpent told Eve that this was a lie, made up by God to stop humans from becoming wise. One could argue that Adam and Eve did not physically die on that day, and so God had therefore lied. However, not only was physical death introduced on that day – God said to Adam, *'For dust you are, and to dust you shall return'* (Genesis 3:19) – but also a greater loss of life was experienced. On that day Adam and Eve died spiritually, hiding themselves from God, who had created and loved them. We are told, *'through one man sin entered the world, and death through sin'* (Romans 5:12). Conclusively, if Adam had chosen not to sin with Eve, remaining faithful to God's command, then sin and the curse of death would not have taken a foothold upon the earth. Yet, our God remains gracious and kind:

> 'But God demonstrates His own love toward us, in that while we were still sinners, Christ died for us.' (Romans 5:8)

Jesus died for our sins and rose again, overcoming the power of death.

> 'Therefore, as through one man's offense judgment came to all men, resulting in condemnation, even so through one Man's righteous act the free gift came to all men, resulting in justification of life.' (Romans 5:18)

We were all dead in our sin before receiving Christ as our Lord and Saviour, who makes us alive (Ephesians 2:1). Many attempt to gain the promise of eternal life by 'good works'. However, *'by grace you have been saved through faith, and that not of yourselves; it is the gift of God'* (Ephesians 2:8).

Their sin forced Adam and Eve out of the Garden of Eden. Though God had to enforce punishment, He remained gracious towards our first parents, replacing their sewn-up fig leaves with tunics of skin (Genesis 3:21). While man can only hide from his shame, God, for whom nothing is impossible, is more than able to cover our shame and bring us back to a place of wholeness in Jesus Christ. For it is written,

> '... And if anyone sins, we have an Advocate with the Father, Jesus Christ the righteous. And He Himself is the propitiation [the appeasement] for our sins, and not for ours only but also for the whole world.' (1 John 2:1–2)

Therefore, *'If we confess our sins, He is faithful and just to forgive us our sins and to cleanse us from all unrighteousness'* (1 John 1:9). To those who fall in love with Jesus the promise is to be *'arrayed in fine linen, clean and bright, for the fine linen is the righteous acts of the saints'* (Revelation 19:8).

After leaving the Garden of Eden, Adam and Eve had two sons: Cain, meaning 'possession', and Abel, meaning 'vanity'. As adults, Cain slew Abel. When Eve bore a third son to Adam, Eve named him Seth meaning 'substitute', *'for God has appointed another seed for me instead of Abel, whom Cain killed'* (Genesis

4:25). Adam and Eve received restoration through the birth of Seth. We are told, *'Then men began to call on the name of the LORD'* (Genesis 4:26). Perhaps, Adam and Eve were too shocked, distressed and ashamed after the murder of their son, to 'call on the name of the Lord'. Their disobedience brought the curse of death, but little could they predict that the first example of man's mortality would be so strongly emphasised in the murder of one of their children by another of their offspring!

In the birth and life of Seth, there was fresh hope; Adam and Eve were encouraged to believe that God cared for them, for *'all things work together for good to those who love God, to those who are the called according to His purpose'* (Romans 8:28). Adam and Eve had other children after Seth, with Adam living a total of nine hundred and thirty years. Eve's death is not recorded and so we do not know what age she was when she died. Who knows? Maybe woman's need to be secretive about her age began with Eve!!

Personal application

God's plan for godly marital relationships can be seen in Adam and Eve's relationship before the fall. God destined for man and woman to be equal, and in marriage, united, as 'two become one'. He also intended for husband and wife to bear their souls to one another without fear of shame or ridicule. This vision became damaged when Adam and Eve became involved in sin, yet the word of God remains intact to lead us back to godly relationships. Through Adam and Eve's disobedience sin entered the world, defiling man's relationship with one another, with God, and with their environment, with curses now being set upon them. Before the Word of God became man, people looked for redemption from their sin in the ritual of slaughtering animals as appeasement offerings to God. We may now receive full redemption from Christ who sacrificed Himself, once and for all, so that all may be forgiven (Romans 6:10). Every curse upon our lives can be broken because Jesus took every curse upon the tree (Galatians 3:13).

▶ Pray together, asking God to grace you with a godly relationship. Read and meditate on the relationship scriptures mentioned (Genesis 1:26–31; 2:20–25; Ephesians 5:22–33). What is God saying to each of you about your relationship with your spouse? Is there a quickening in your spirit that reveals a wrong attitude towards marriage and your partner? If so, repent of your error, and make a commitment to choose to relate according to your newfound belief. Forgive one another and begin again.

▶ Take time out to be together, away from distractions. (Don't let phone calls take priority over your relationship.) Dress to impress your partner, just as you would have done before marriage. Be completely honest with one another, but not brutal – you don't want to be responsible for breaking your partner's spirit! Agree to make changes, and work towards fulfilling the promises that *you* make. Learn to express yourselves freely with one another, sharing your hopes and dreams, concerns and fears, for the two of you have become one! You may ask, 'Why go to all this bother?' The answer was aptly given to me by a friend – 'If you don't work at the relationship, the relationship won't work!'

▶ Praying to remove curses is relatively easy, as long as you have invited Jesus into your life, have a personal relationship with Him and believe in the authority you have in His name. In the Acts of the Apostles, we are told of the authority that Jesus' disciples took over demons, but when people who did not know Jesus attempted to cast out demons in His name, the demons attacked them (Acts 19:13–17).

Firstly, for those who would like to begin a personal relationship with Jesus Christ, this simple prayer could be said:

> *Lord Jesus,*
> *I am sorry for the things that I have done wrong in my life. I ask for Your forgiveness and now turn from everything that I know is wrong. Thank You for dying on the cross for me to set me free from my sins. Please come into my life, fill me with Your Holy Spirit, and be with me forever. Thank You Lord Jesus. Amen.*

Secondly, a simple prayer to set people free from a curse might be as follows:

> *Lord Jesus,*
> *You died on the cross to set me free from every curse. Therefore, I no longer accept the curse of Eve over my womb. I/we break this curse in the name of Jesus Christ, the Son of God. And I/we*

pray blessings over my womb [be specific, commanding period pains to be gone, menstrual tension to disappear, the womb to become fruitful or peaceful. Where there is no womb, pray for Jesus to fill the barrenness, physical, spiritual, and/or emotional emptiness]. *I/We pray this in Jesus' name. Amen.*

I must mention here that breaking the curse of Eve over another lady's life gained only partial healing. The key to full healing was the repenting of vows she had made over her sexuality because of sexual abuse that she had suffered. Others in the same situation should ask the Holy Spirit to reveal ungodly vows that are holding them in bondage to pain, and repent of them to be set free. Alleluia!

Find another Christian, if you can, to pray the prayers in agreement with you. However, if there is no one available, the Lord will gladly be your 'prayer partner'. Speak to Him and He shall surely respond!

▶ Consider a family or ministry Sabbath-day rest. When the Sabbath rest was instigated, the Israelites were told to rest together, even the foreign slaves were not to work (Exodus 20:8–11); the spirit of rest hovering over the home brings peace and invigoration.

What things should we do on the Sabbath? God says *'keep it holy'* (Deuteronomy 5:12). The two most important commandments God gives are honouring God above everything else and loving others as we love ourselves (Matthew 22:37–40). These are commandments we should always work at fulfilling, and on the Sabbath, when all other work is set aside, we have a greater opportunity to bring a godly focus into relationships. Socialising, then, is an important part of the Sabbath rest; playing games with your kids, listening to one another, taking time out together. A practical element of the Sabbath rest is providing for our rest in advance. As the Israelites in the desert collected their Sabbath food on the preceding day (Exodus 16:22–23), we also need to prepare meals to avoid unnecessarily busyness.

Chapter 3
Brother's Keeper: Cain and Abel

Cain and Abel, sons of Adam and Eve, were introduced by their occupations; Abel was a shepherd and Cain a farmer. In time, they each brought an offering before the Lord, Cain bringing *'an offering of the fruit of the ground'* (Genesis 4:3) and Abel bringing *'of the firstborn of his flock and of their fat'* (Genesis 4:5).

> *'... And the LORD respected Abel and his offering, but He did not respect Cain and His offering ...'* (Genesis 4:4–5)

Genesis doesn't say why the Lord respected one offering above the other. As both types of sacrifice are acceptable gifts to the Lord (Numbers 18:12, 17), we can conclude that Cain's attitude, rather than his offering, displeased God.

The writer of Hebrews tells us *'By faith Abel offered to God a more excellent sacrifice than Cain'* (Hebrews 11:4). How was this so? Abel brought a living sacrifice, presumably a lamb, which throughout the history of the Jewish people has been used as a 'sin offering' sacrifice to appease God. Instructions on how to carry out a sin offering were given to the priests of God in Leviticus (Leviticus 4:34), with the sinner receiving forgiveness through the blood of the lamb (Leviticus 4:35). Abel, therefore, was acknowledging his sin and seeking God's forgiveness. Jesus referred to Abel as one of the prophets whose blood was shed (Luke 11:50–51).

Cain brought a gift of thanksgiving, an acceptable part of worship, but not enough on its own. Cain was expressing a 'religious spirit' in his belief that he did not need to acknowledge his own sinfulness or seek the mercy of God. Jesus spoke of Cain's hypocritical attitude in the parable of 'The Pharisee and the Tax Collector' (Luke 18:9–14). The Pharisee gave an oracle of thanks to God for his own good behaviour while the tax collector pleaded, *'God be merciful to me a sinner!'* (Luke 18:13). Jesus concludes, *'this man went down to his house justified rather than the other; for everyone who exalts himself will be abased and he who humbles himself will be exalted'* (Luke 18:14). Cain, in realising that Abel's sacrifice was accepted above his, became very angry:

> *'So the* Lord *said to Cain, "Why are you angry? And why has your countenance fallen? If you do well, will you not be accepted?" ... '* (Genesis 4:6–7)

God encouraged Cain that he too would be accepted by admitting his own sinfulness and need for forgiveness. The Lord, knowing Cain's character, also warned,

> *' ... And if you do not do well, sin lies at the door. And its desire is for you, but you should rule over it.'* (Genesis 4:7)

If we will not take this first step towards redemption, then sin will take over our lives; in not admitting our own sinfulness, we find justification to live as we please. God warns all of us that Satan, the tempter, would have sin reign over us, but that we must rule over sin and not allow ourselves to fall prey to temptation. God tells us that we need to make a conscious decision to rule over sin, destroying the notion that one cannot help oneself from sinning. Of course, we cannot succeed alone. *'Resist the devil and he will flee'* (James 4:7) is not a command that stands alone, depending on our own strength. Firstly, we are called to *'submit to God'* (James 4:7). Then, under the protection and direction of Almighty God, we are able to resist the devil and he will surely flee!

Cain, however, chose not to submit to God nor resist the devil, but rather opted to 'lash out' in anger towards his brother:

> *'Now Cain talked with Abel his brother; and it came to pass, when they were in the field, that Cain rose against Abel his brother and killed him.'* (Genesis 4:8)

The Greek, Samaritan, and other ancient versions, add that Cain said to his brother, 'Let us go into the field', deceptively talking and walking with Abel in 'friendship', in order to exact revenge.

When God asked Cain where his brother was, Cain chose to continue the road of deception replying, *'I do not know. Am I my brother's keeper?'* (Genesis 4:9). Cain killed without legitimate justification and then denied any knowledge of Abel's death. Obviously, we cannot keep the truth from God and yet, there is in man a pride that is willing to attempt to do so! Cain even went as far as to give a rhetorical response, 'Am I my brother's keeper?' A keeper could also be referred to as a guardian, caretaker, custodian, guard, or preserver. Surely, as an older brother, Cain was expected to preserve and care for his younger brother's life. Instead, he became the first murderer, taking his brother's life without a cause. John, in the New Testament writings, declares Cain to have been *'of the wicked one'* who chose to murder Abel because *'his works were evil and his brother's righteous'* (1 John 3:12). One questions how Cain dared to speak to God with such contempt. It reveals the truth that rebellion hardens the heart (Psalm 95:8).

God continued,

> *'... The voice of your brother's blood cries out to Me from the ground.'* (Genesis 4:10)

God gave life to Abel, and Cain dared to supersede God's authority by taking it away, but *'the life of the flesh is in the blood'* (Leviticus 17:11) and so even from the grave, the blood of Abel cried out to God for justice. Cain's punishment was his being cursed from the earth, becoming a fugitive and a vagabond (Genesis 4:11–12). Cain still did not consider his sin, but considered it fitting to complain to God, *My punishment is greater than I can bear! ... I shall be hidden from your face ... anyone who finds me will kill me'* (Genesis 4:13–14). Sin indeed 'hides' us from the face of God; not knowing our place of belonging in Him, we are uncertain of His love and protection. I hate the times when Satan has won the battle and I have sinned. Shame forces me to retreat from God, yet God's mercy beckons me to draw close, repent and be forgiven, and be healed and set free to begin again. Cain, however, was only able to recognise the consequence of God's punishment, not the consequence of his own sin. Throughout the Bible when man repented, God mercifully forgave. Cain was too self-centred to even comprehend a need for repentance and instead asked for a 'fairer' sentence. God obliged, promising,

> '... "whoever kills Cain, vengeance shall be taken on him sevenfold." And the LORD set a mark on Cain, lest anyone finding him should kill him.' (Genesis 4:15)

No one knows what the mark was upon Cain, but we can be certain it was an obvious warning, for anyone who was tempted to harm Cain, to reconsider!

'*Then Cain went out from the presence of the* LORD' (Genesis 4:16), is arguably one of the saddest verses in the Bible. God is always merciful, but that doesn't make Him a 'soft touch'; we can either choose to live in His Kingdom, by His Kingdom rules, or walk away from His covering. Unfortunately, Cain chose the latter option, departing to live in the land of Nod, meaning 'the land of a vagabond'. His wife, whose name is not given, bore Cain at least one son. Cain's genealogy is recorded in Genesis 4. Amongst them are many talented people: the father of all who dwell in tents and have livestock, the father of all who play the harp and flute, and an instructor of every craftsman in bronze and iron. Sadly, however, none of his posterity are recorded as having a relationship with God.

Personal application

Cain and Abel's different offerings revealed opposing heart attitudes towards God:

> '*By faith Abel offered to God a more excellent sacrifice than Cain.*' (Hebrews 11:4)

Cain, having a religious spirit, was unable to recognise his need for repentance or God's forgiveness, and offered a gift without faith. His sin led him to greater sin – from disobedience to murder.

- Read the account of Cain and Abel's lives (Genesis 4:1–15). Those around us judge our actions, but God judges our hearts. Allow the Holy Spirit to reveal to you any hypocrisy in your offerings to Him. Do you judge the profoundness of the occasion by the amount you have given instead of the depth of God's mercy and love? Have you been following your own agenda, perhaps hoping to gain respect in the church instead of deepening your relationship with Jesus? Repent of the error that the Holy Spirit reveals to you, and choose to place your faith in God, giving thanks and praise to Him for bringing you into freedom.

Chapter 4
Family Traits: Seth and Enoch vs. Cain and Lamech

The 'Promised Seed', the Messiah, could not come through Cain or Abel because of Cain's sin, and so God fulfilled His promise through a third son, Seth, who brought fresh hope and vision for *'Then men began to call on the name of the* Lord*'* (Genesis 4:26). God remains faithful even when we are not!

Comparing the family traits of Seth and Cain in the lives of their respective descendants Enoch and Lamech, we are given a vivid account of the law of generational blessing and curse (Deuteronomy 28). Our faithfulness to God is rewarded by family blessings, whilst sinful behaviour gives authority over to Satan to curse our family line. Enoch, as a descendant of Seth, inherited faithfulness and integrity, whilst Lamech inherited self-righteousness, pride, and vengefulness from Cain. Put simply, we might describe it as 'like father, like son'. In accordance with this definition, Lamech honoured himself for killing a young man who had merely struck him (Genesis 4:23). Past generations' sins cannot excuse our own sinful behaviour. We always have personal choice; realising we gravitate towards the sins of our forefathers will help us to recognise our personal battlefield. In Christ Jesus, every curse can be turned into a blessing,

> *'Christ has redeemed us from the curse of the law, having become a curse for us (for it is written, "Cursed is everyone who hangs on a tree").'* (Galatians 3:13)

To be set free from generational curses we need to repent, on behalf of our forefathers, for the sin committed, asking for God's forgiveness and speaking forgiveness over our generation line.

We must make a decision to allow God to be Lord of that area of our lives. For example, alcohol abuse is in my family line. While other Christians may be free to drink alcohol, the Lord has asked me to abstain, as much for my family's sake as my own. Being of the world, they do not readily recognise their enslavement to alcohol, but I trust God to set them free in His time. Amen!

Lamech, like his father Cain, chose to sin and then presumptuously demanded the mercy of God to protect him:

> *'If Cain shall be avenged sevenfold,*
> *Then Lamech seventy-sevenfold.'* (Genesis 4:24)

This brings about the question – can we expect God's blessing because we announce it? Surely a scripture that I claim over my life by my self-will cannot have the same power as when God promises it. Paul told the Philippians that God would provide their need from their own account of generous giving (Philippians 4:15–19). If I declare that God will provide all my needs *'according to His riches'* (Philippians 4:19), but do not fulfil the prerequisite, how can I expect God to fulfil the promise to me? We need to live in relation to both the Spirit and Word of God.

We know so much about the sin of Lamech whilst knowing comparatively little about Enoch; he had sons and daughters and *'walked with God; and he was not, for God took him'* (Genesis 5:24). We glean from Enoch the importance of life – a relationship with God.

> *'By faith Enoch was taken away so that he did not see death, "and was not found because God had taken him"; for before he was taken he had this testimony, that he pleased God.'*
> (Hebrews 11:5)

He walked with God and as he walked, God took him! Beautiful!

Personal application

The Bible breaks from the list of descendants in the seventh generation of both Seth and Cain to give examples of blessings and curses on the family line. Be encouraged to know that we can break curses, that have been passed down our generation line, by the cross of Jesus, and as we live in faithful relationship with the Lord, that we are bringing blessings upon future generations. Here is a prayer to break the power of curses on your generation line:

> *Dear Father,*
> *I repent on behalf of my forefathers for sins that they have committed, resulting in curses upon the family line. I ask Your forgiveness over them and I choose to forgive them. I also ask You to forgive me for committing sin. I forgive myself. Jesus took the curse upon the tree, and so I need no longer live under its power. I break the power of the curse of* [name them – addiction, abuse, violence, rejection, etc.] *over my life and the lives of my family, and choose to walk in the freedom of Christ. Amen!*

Everything that is of importance can be seen in the recording of Enoch's life; put your relationship with God above everything else, and everything else will fall into place. When we attempt, in our own strength, to love our 'unlovable' neighbour as we love ourselves, we become frustrated with our constant failings. However, when we spend time in the presence of Almighty God, who *is* Love, allowing Him to shares with us His heart, we are filled with a genuine love that enables us to live according to God's command (Matthew 19:19).

Chapter 5

Float On! Noah and the Lord

Noah belonged to the tenth generation of man. Sadly, after only ten generations upon the earth, man had become so wicked that,

> '... *every intent of the thoughts of his heart was only evil continually. And the* LORD *was sorry that He had made man on the earth and He was grieved in His heart.*' (Genesis 6:5–6)

It was not that some of man's thoughts had evil intent, but that their every thought was evil and the continuous bombardment of wickedness upon the earth was grieving God (Genesis 6:11). I imagine that it would have been quite a fearful time to be alive; if all were corrupt who could be trusted, and if all were violent then what hopes were there of peace?

One could ask, 'How did man, sinful as he was, become so degenerative?' The answer may be,

> '*that the sons of God saw the daughters of men, that they were beautiful; and they took wives for themselves of all whom they chose.*' (Genesis 6:2)

With various suggestions on the meaning of this verse, the one most credible to me is that the *'sons of God'* were the seed of Seth, men who had previously called on the name of the Lord, and the *'daughters of men'* were seed from Cain, people who followed carnal desires. This union of the *'sons of God'* with the unrighteous seed of Cain could only result in one thing; the righteous seed of Seth would become corrupt. For we are warned, *'Do not be deceived: "Evil company corrupts good habits"'* (1 Corinthians 15:33). In order to remain pure, the children of God must *'not be unequally yoked with unbelievers. For what fellowship has righteousness with lawlessness?'* (2 Corinthians 6:14). Yet, man did not want to be received by God, choosing instead to fulfil the desires of the flesh.

God decided to destroy man whom He had created, *'But Noah found grace in the eyes of the Lord'* (Genesis 6:8). Noah, like his ancestor, Enoch, *'walked with God'*, being *'a just man, perfect in his generations'* (Genesis 6:9). God shared with Noah His grief over man's evil ways, and His plan to destroy them and every living thing that they had been given authority over. The Lord desires to share His heart and His intentions with His children; He searches for a people who have the integrity to be His friends. When we observe biblical characters such as Noah, we often presume that they were 'super holy', having qualities that we couldn't attain to. However, the Bible doesn't suggest so. Noah chose to 'walk with God', but it was God's grace which carried him! Noah, like Paul the apostle, would say, *'By the grace of God I am what I am'* (1 Corinthians 15:10).

The Lord also shared with Noah what he had to do to save his family; he was to build an ark to God's specific directions and receive a number of living creatures, again to God's specific requirements. The Lord declared to Noah that He would bring a flood of water upon the earth to destroy all living things,

> *'But I will establish My covenant with you; and you shall go into the ark – you, your sons, your wife, and your son's wives with you.'* (Genesis 6:18)

The psalmist shares,

> *'The secret of the Lord is with those who fear* [revere] *Him, And He will show them His covenant.'* (Psalm 25:14)

For

> *'Good and upright is the Lord; Therefore He teaches sinners in the way.'* (Psalm 25:8)

If we wish to receive God's blessings, then we need to be obedient to His voice.

> *'Thus, Noah did; according to all that God commanded him, so he did.'* (Genesis 6:22)

The Lord said to Noah,

> *'Make yourself an ark of gopherwood; make rooms in the ark, and cover it inside and outside with pitch ... The length of the ark shall be three hundred cubits, its width fifty cubits, and its height thirty cubits ... You shall make it with lower, second, and third decks.'* (Genesis 6:14, 15, 16)

The discovery of Hezekiah's channel, mentioned in 2 Kings 20:20, makes it possible to know the length of the cubit in modern terms – one and a half feet or half a metre. If the 'cubit' was the same size in Noah's day as in Hezekiah's, his ark was one hundred and fifty metres long, twenty-five metres wide, and fifteen metres high. That's quite a large construction, able to hold eighteen of today's largest ships! Such a construction was going to take time and labour to complete. Genesis does not tell us directly how many years, or people it took to build the ark, but we can presume that if Noah did not employ neighbours in its construction, then they would certainly have been aware of its growing presence!

We can glean from New Testament writers a sense of the spiritual atmosphere whilst the ark was being built. God was willing to save as many as would repent of disobedience; *'the Divine longsuffering waited in the days of Noah, while the ark was being prepared'* (1 Peter 3:20). Noah warned the people of the wrath to come, and preached salvation to them as he was *'a preacher of righteousness'* (2 Peter 2:5). Jesus tells us that the people chose to take no notice of Noah's warning for,

> *'They ate, they drank, they married wives, they were given in marriage, until the day that Noah entered the ark, and the flood came and destroyed them all.'* (Luke 17:27)

It need not have been so, for we learn from Jonah's experience that when the people repented of their wicked ways *'God relented from the disaster that He had said He would bring upon them, and He did not do it'* (Jonah 3:10).

The day eventually came for Noah and his family to go into the ark. Perhaps the day appeared to be like any other, with no signs of a forthcoming storm, for it was not the weather Noah followed but the voice of the Lord. Just as exercise strengthens the body, God strengthens our spirits by encouraging us to walk by faith. Having had a call to Morocco, friends of mine, John and Penny, obediently sold everything in South Africa and moved to the UK for God to show them the next step. No immediate connection comes to mind between Morocco and Britain, yet God had planned for them to pastor the Anglican Church (Church of England!) in Casablanca. Penny, in a dream, saw the church that they were to minister in, which they later found out was in desperate need of a leader; God was waiting for them to take up the position that He had created for them! So too, Noah was told to enter the ark with his family and the animals that God had brought to him to preserve, seven days before *'the waters of the flood were on the earth'* (Genesis 7:10).

> *'So those that entered, male and female of all flesh, went in as God had commanded him* [Noah]; *and the* LORD *shut him in.'*
> (Genesis 7:16)

The *Lord* shut Noah in. Noah built the door, but God shut it! God, not man, must execute the fulfilment of God's warning. For Noah to close the door of salvation on his neighbours, to leave them to drown, would have been far too great a responsibility for any man. However, our God is a just God; Noah's family saw for themselves how many times God was prepared to rescue the people from their sin, but that they were always unwilling. God was justified in 'starting again', and Noah and his family were blessed to be a part of this 'new beginning'.

Throughout the Old Testament, there are 'types' for New Testament revelations. A 'type' is a thing that represents something else or is intended to foreshow it. Noah's ark was a type of Christ Jesus, and the flood was a type of the future destruction of the world. Noah and his family were saved by faith; by faith, they believed God and entered the ark. All who, by faith, choose to enter into relationship with Jesus Christ, our Saviour, will receive salvation from the destruction that awaits those who choose to remain in disobedience. In the same way as Noah and his family were invited to begin again with God, the Lord invites each of us to be 'born again', for

> *'... according to His mercy He saved us, through the washing of regeneration and renewing of the Holy Spirit, whom He poured out on us abundantly through Jesus Christ our Savior, that having*

been justified by His grace we should become heirs according to the hope of eternal life.' (Titus 3:5–7)

The ark was a preservation box, with every animal departing as healthy as it entered. This called for another 'step of faith' as the family were to care for the animals, but also to trust their continued existence to God; for if one of a pair should die then that species would become extinct. As in the Garden of Eden, Adam and Eve did not bear children; neither people nor animals had young with them in the ark. I see this as the grace of God in action. The ark may have been large, but it was still a confined space! This lengthy journey was not the time for Noah's daughters-in-law to bear or raise children, and so God closed their wombs until the appropriate time. As it is written, *'sons were born to them* [the sons of Noah] *after the flood'* (Genesis 10:1).

The Lord shared with Noah His plan to *'cause it to rain on the earth forty days and forty nights'* (Genesis 7:4). Having not, however, shared with Noah how long the waters would remain upon the earth, the family perhaps felt abandoned, seeing no change in the water level. This happens in our own lives; God gives us enough information to have us embark on a journey, but during it He doesn't seem to confide in us, as much as we would like. When I returned to England from Kenya for one month, I was shocked to realise that I could not return as I had intended. Jesus told me to ring a friend, who amazingly had a room available for two months. I often asked the Lord 'what next?' but He refused to tell me, instead teaching me to wait. Then a request came from a friend; could I pop over to Morocco for a few weeks to take care of her children while she was in America. I knew this was God's calling, and was blessed not only to 'be there' for two wonderful children, but, as my three week trip turned into eight months, I also taught in the American School and became deeply involved in the local church.

So too, after five months in the ark and seeing a change in the weather, the family were gratefully aware that God *'remembered'* their situation (Genesis 8:1). However, if they considered this the end of their journey, they would have been mistaken. The journey in total was to last just over a year. I wonder what lessons of faith the 'sailors' learnt, for while such times of waiting seem tedious to us, God will use them to mould in us godly attributes of *'love, joy, peace, longsuffering, kindness, goodness, faithfulness, gentleness, self-control'* (Galatians 5:22–23), if only we allow Him! After all, this little group of people were important in God's plan; as the whole world was to be populated through them, they needed to know and trust God intimately.

Towards the end of their journey, the ark having become stationary on the mountains of Ararat, Noah began to test the remaining water level by sending out birds. The raven, able to survive on floating carcasses, never returned, but the account of the relationship between Noah and the dove is so beautifully poetic: *'The dove found no resting place for the sole of her foot.'* And so, she flew back to Noah, who *'put out his hand and took her, and drew her into the ark to himself'* (Genesis 8:9). Remember that the ark is a type for Jesus. Consider this then – when you or I can find no rest, we can turn to Jesus Christ who will lovingly and consistently put out His hand and draw us into the depth of His own heart. For our Lord says to each of us,

> *'Come to Me, all you who labor and are heavy laden, and I will give you rest. Take My yoke upon you and learn from Me, for I am gentle and lowly in heart, and you will find rest for your souls.'*
> (Matthew 11:28–29)

The second time that Noah sent the dove out she returned in the evening with a freshly plucked olive leaf, revealing that the floods had not only gone from the earth, but that vegetation had begun to grow. For the dove to pluck an olive leaf there had to be an olive branch (a resting place!). On her first expedition, the dove found no resting place and so, out of necessity, returned to Noah. However, this time she chose to return to share her findings. Noah trusted the dove to work with him and she proved faithful to his expectation. Our relationship with Jesus should be just the same, for faith without works is dead (James 2:17). Some time later, Noah removed the covering of the ark and found the ground to be dry, yet he and his family remained in the ark. Noah's assessments were for information rather than direction, for as Noah obeyed God in entering the ark, he chose to remain there until God told him to depart.

> *'Then Noah built an altar to the* Lord *...'*   (Genesis 8:20)

In everything, our praise and adoration should to be to God! Noah could not steer the ark, and our Lord God had guided them safely to the mountaintops; we should also thank God for His protection. Noah and his family were privileged to be chosen as the family who were to 'begin again' with God; we need to recognise and appreciate God's grace in our lives too! In this new setting, Noah and his family did not know what course their lives would take – we also always need to seek God's direction and blessing in new ventures!

> 'So God blessed Noah and his sons, and said to them: "Be fruitful and multiply, and fill the earth."' (Genesis 9:1)

Personal application

Noah walked with God, and was considered a 'just man'. God did not invite Noah to walk with Him because he was upright, but rather Noah increased in virtue as he walked with God, with God's character rubbing off on him. The Lord invites each of us to do the same.

- ▶ To walk with God we need to make a daily commitment to spend time with Him. New Christians may find waiting to hear God's voice a struggle, and mature Christians may have accidentally got so overly involved in the work of the Lord, that they no longer have time for the Lord of the work! However, God desires to share His heart's desire with you – plans for you, your family, your work place, your neighbourhood, and even world events.

- ▶ On agreeing to spend time with God, set a realistic goal for yourself – when is the best time each day for you to sit in God's presence, and how long can you stay?

- ▶ Write down your appointment in your diary or calendar and plan to keep it, just as you would keep any other appointment.

- ▶ Begin your time in God's presence by meditating on His word,

  > 'For I know the thoughts that I think toward you, says the LORD, thoughts of peace and not of evil, to give you a future and a hope.' (Jeremiah 29:11)

- Keep a journal, noting God's words to you. If you're unsure if it's God's word, write it down anyway. As you mature in Christ and look back, you will have greater discernment to recognise God's thoughts, as opposed to your own 'good ideas'.
- Trust God to continue speaking to you as a friend.

Chapter 6
World Leaders: Noah's Sons

Before leaving the ark we knew nothing of Noah's sons, except that they were married and were considered righteous enough by God to live. Then, we are given their names – Shem, Ham, and Japheth. We are told, in preparation for later conflicts, that Ham was the father of Canaan.

In those days, Noah planted a vineyard. Noah got drunk from his wine,

> '... and became uncovered in his tent. And Ham, the father of Canaan, saw the nakedness of his father, and told his two brothers outside.' (Genesis 9:21–22)

They then went into their father's tent, walking backwards and covered him, without looking on their father's nakedness. When Noah awoke, he knew what his son, Ham, had done to him and cursed Ham's son, Canaan, to become a servant of servants, serving Shem and Japheth (Genesis 9:24–25). What sin had Ham committed to receive such a severe punishment? Biblical language is often lost in translation; just as 'knowing' someone is a reference to sexual intercourse, 'seeing someone's nakedness' can refer to a lustful look or action (Ezekiel 22:10). Scripture says Noah, even though he had been drunk, knew what Ham had done to him, and it shamed him enough to curse Ham's descendants. Many children become their parents' carers in later life, as I have done, and some I know fear that they inevitably take a curse upon themselves in caring for, and therefore seeing, their parents' nakedness. God judges the intent of the heart, and the person who respectfully cares for a parent's physical needs is honouring that parent and therefore keeping the commandment of God. This, in turn, brings the blessing of long life

(Exodus 20:12), and not a curse as Ham's sin incurred upon his descendants.

> 'These three were the sons of Noah, and from these the whole earth was populated.' (Genesis 9:19)

> 'Blessed be the LORD,
> The God of Shem.' (Genesis 9:26)

From Shem descended the Jews, God's chosen people, with Abraham being of the eighth generation of Shem (Genesis 11:10–26). So too, the Jews are aware that the Messiah must come through this generation line, but many are sadly blind to the fact that He has already come and that His name is Jesus Christ the Lord. Noah also blessed his son, Japheth, through whom the lands of the Gentiles were blessed (Genesis 10:5). Noah prayed,

> 'May god enlarge Japheth,
> And may he dwell in the tents of Shem ... ' (Genesis 9:27)

This can be seen as a prophecy of the conversion of the Gentiles, the sewing on of a wild branch to the tree of life, granting us the blessings of becoming sons of God. The descendants of Ham were cursed to slavery – a servant of servants, despised by his brethren. They were to be a people who inhabited the continent of Africa, and throughout history, this prophecy has sadly been fulfilled, often under the dominion of an alien power. This can be seen in such empires as the Romans in Jesus' day, to European countries in modern times, such as Africans being barbarously oppressed and even bought and sold like animals in the marketplace. But in Jesus, we can all experience the blessing of salvation; both individual and country can escape this curse as they take on their new identity in Christ – Jesus Himself, took the curse upon the cross and justifies each one of us, in His resurrection, to walk in the blessings of inheritance in Christ.

Personal application

The three sons of Noah populated the whole world. Through Ham's behaviour, a curse descended on a whole nation; this reveals how the behaviour of previous generations has spiritual repercussions. Similar to breaking family-line curses, we need to recognise that in Jesus we can be set free from the curse, repenting on behalf of previous generations, forgiving them, and praying blessings upon the people of our land. Parliament passing ungodly laws has undoubtedly brought curses upon our land; if you allow people to murder members of an unborn generation, you can expect that generation to pick up the spirit of violence, and so violence and murder becomes more commonplace in society.

- Before embarking on spiritual warfare, make sure you are wearing your armour – the belt of truth, body-jacket of righteousness, shoes of peace, and most importantly, the shield of faith, helmet of salvation and the sword that is the Word of God (Ephesians 6:10–18). This is not to be confused with physical armour that is removed when not at war, for Christ's army must always be prepared. Check your armour daily to make sure you're wearing it properly (e.g. claiming to have the sword in your hand when you never meditate on God's Word will leave you without a weapon to fight with!).

- Pray to break curses over your nations. This following prayer can also be adapted to pray for other nations that the Lord places on your heart:

    Dear Jesus,
    We bring our nation before You. Forgive us for the sins that we have committed, including ungodly laws that we have instigated. Turn the hearts of the nation to You so that we may live according to Your Word. We speak authority in Your name, breaking the power of curses over our nation, and ask You not to hold us guilty for the sins of our forefathers, but to set us free as we speak blessings over our nation in Your name [speak peace where there has been violence, prosperity where there has been poverty, godly freedom where there has been oppression, etc.]. *We pray for those in authority, that they may make decisions in accordance with Your teaching, bringing blessings upon our nation. Amen!*

- Pray to break curses over individuals:

    Lord God,
    We bring before You [name] *who is from* [country]. *We come against any authority that Satan has had to force curses upon*

him/her because of the country of his/her origin. We declare that he/she is bought with a price, delivered from the power of darkness, and is now a citizen of the Kingdom of God, receiving the rich blessings set aside for the children of God [Colossians 1:13]. *We therefore break the curse of* [poverty, inferiority, etc.] *upon* [name's] *life, and pray rich blessings of Almighty God into his/her life. Amen!*

Chapter 7
Friend and Confidant: Abraham and the Lord

Abraham was born Abram, son of Terah, in Ur of the Chaldeans, after the Lord scattered the people all over the earth and confused their language (Genesis 11:1–9). Ironically, the people of Babel designed 'a tower reaching to heaven' to protect themselves from dispersion. When we attempt to protect and provide excessively for ourselves, be it due to fear or pride, we instantly come out of the blessing of protection and provision from Almighty God, setting ourselves up against God's power and authority.

It had not taken humanity long after the flood to become degenerate beings, and even Terah, Abram's father, worshipped foreign gods (Joshua 24:2). Yet, God did not become so exasperated with the antics of humanity that He would give up on us completely, but rather began to relate to His creation through one man, Abraham, and his descendants.

> 'Now, the Lord had said to Abram:
>
>> "Get out of your country,
>> From your kindred
>> And from your father's house,
>> To a land that I will show you.
>> I will make you a great nation;
>> I will bless you
>> And make your name great;
>> And you shall be a blessing.
>> I will bless those who bless you,
>> And I will curse him who curses you;
>> And in you all families of the earth will be blessed."'
>
> (Genesis 12:1–3)

Abram was seventy-five years old and childless when God spoke these words to him. The promises were *big*, but these promises would only be fulfilled if Abram complied with the conditions set down by God; that Abraham should leave his old life behind and the security it brought, and follow God's direction to a new land – a new security designed by God.

Abram obeyed immediately! He departed *'as the Lord had spoken to him'* (Genesis 12:4). When God says 'Let's go', or 'Get out', there needs to be an obedient response – or do we claim that for some reason Abram was able to hear God's voice more clearly than we do in the 21st century? Of course we need to be sure it's God, and so it may be appropriate to ask Him for confirmation, but we also have to believe that we have the same ability to discern the voice of God as Abram had. He was introduced to us as the son of Terah, nothing else; he was not a man of great faith or close friendship with God, yet still he heard God and obeyed. The characteristic that set him apart was his willingness to obey the voice of God. Today, our God is both willing and desiring to set apart and bless those who will hear His voice and obey His commands.

As Abram travelled through the land of Canaan with his wife Sarai, his nephew Lot, and their servants, the Lord appeared to Abram, and said, *'To your descendants I will give this land'* (Genesis 12:7a). This was an amazing revelation! Abram was travelling through a foreign land, perhaps feeling a little weary from the journey, when the Lord encouraged him with 'Look around you, son, this is the land I promised you.' God's first word spoken to Abram required immediate action, thus Abram began travelling without knowing his destination. This second spoken word needed acknowledgment of God's promise and worship of the God who is faithful to His promises; *'and there he built an altar to the Lord, who had appeared to him'* (Genesis 12:7b).

A severe famine came upon the land and so Abram decided to go down to Egypt, with his family, *'to sojourn there'* (Genesis 12:10). The Lord had told Abram that He was giving him and his descendants the land of Canaan, yet here he was choosing to leave. Would you know the right thing to do? Would you begin to question whether you've followed the voice of God or an over-active imagination? Was the arduous journey thus far God-directed, and therefore a blessing, or could you have submitted the family to aimless trudging through a great wilderness? It is at crucial points like this that we are forced to 'face reality'. We may feel confused and abandoned, emotions that none of us care to experience, but as we face up to the emotions by bringing them before the Lord and seek His understanding of the situation, we become more secure in His promises and more certain of His direction. It is a good thing to be able to let go of God's promises to the Lord in order to receive a fresh, deeper revelation from Him. Had Abram chosen to return to his native homeland during the famine, he would not have been so much letting go as giving in. Once home, it would have been easier to accept 'home comforts' rather than choose to step out again in faith to receive God's promises. God's promises would never have been realised – and that's a scary thought, not just for Abram, but also for every family of the world! The proof that Abram believed it was God's direction to move to Egypt was that his intention was not to settle there, but to 'sojourn' (dwell temporarily) in Egypt. Therefore, as he travelled towards Egypt, he was sure of God's promise to return him to Canaan where he would become a great nation. When God has spoken, His promises will come to pass at the appointed time. I have a friend who knew early in life that she had a calling to Africa, but she had to wait decades for the opportunity to materialise. She has realised many times that the Lord used every 'detour' to prepare her for the work.

As Abram approached Egypt he was overcome with fear that the Egyptians may have tried to kill him to take his beautiful wife. Hadn't Abram forgotten something? – All of God's promises! He promised to make him a great nation and to fight his battles for him. God had great plans for Abram, which could not be fulfilled if the Egyptians had the power and authority to kill him. Abram had been able to obey when the Lord first spoke these promises to him, but perhaps with time, his faith dwindled. Abram introduced Sarai as his sister and exchanged her with Pharaoh for great wealth. With amazing insight, Pharaoh realised that a curse that was upon him was the result of having Abram's wife, and rebuked Abram, returned Sarai to him and commanded that he be sent away with his wife and all that he had (Genesis 12:20). God used Abram's weakness to bless him, leaving Egypt *'very rich in livestock, in silver, and in gold'* (Genesis 13:2). To become a great nation, one needs great wealth.

Abram travelled far back:

> *'to the place of the altar which he had made there at first. And there Abram called on the name of the* LORD.*'* (Genesis 13:4)

Sometimes, when we've confused matters with human reasoning, and dealt with issues in our own strength rather than under the grace and direction of God, we need to go back to the beginning – to the place where we know we heard God's voice – and stay in that place until we know and are sure of His direction once again. When we have failed, though humans may reject us, the Lord will always receive us and give us the comfort we need. As we return to the Lord in our time of need, He would say to us,

> '... *I will not forget you.*
> *See, I have inscribed you on the palms of My hands* ...'
> (Isaiah 49:15–16)

While Abram remained in that place disputes began between his herdsmen and Lot's herdsmen for

> '... *the land was not able to support them, that they might dwell together, for their possessions were so great* ...' (Genesis 13:6)

Abram, not wanting to fall out with his nephew over the problem, suggested that they should divide the land between them, allowing Lot the first choice. Lot responding immediately and *'lifted his eyes and saw all the plains of Jordan, that it was well watered everywhere'* (Genesis 13:10). As a result, he chose for himself all the plain of Jordan, and departed from his uncle. How must Abram have felt? Having sacrificed much to keep the peace, was he saddened by Lot's quick and self-absorbent response?

In the sad moments of change, when we are forced to let go, we will often hear our Lord speaking to us with new and precious revelations that will change our lives.

> '*And the* LORD *said to Abram* ... "*Lift your eyes now and look from the place where you are – northward, southward, eastward, and westward; for all the land which you see I give to you and your descendants forever.*"' (Genesis 13:14–15)

Lot may have chosen the most sumptuous land to dwell in, but God had said that it was an inheritance for Abram and his descendants. So far, the word 'descendant' recorded in Scripture could mean 'one born in your family', but here the Lord used a word which is literally translated 'seed'. Lot had been brought up in Abram's home and so was presumably like a son to him.

Perhaps Abram needed to physically release his nephew in order for him to realise that God would not fulfil His promises to Abram through Lot, but would actually give Abram 'seed' of his own. The Lord goes so far as to promise:

> *'And I will make your descendants as the dust of the earth; so that if a man could number the dust of the earth, then your descendants also could be numbered.'* (Genesis 13:16)

Remembering that Abram was seventy-five years old when he began his journey, and he had not yet produced any children, this is a mighty, miraculous promise from the Lord! Would you believe it? The mind battles with the outlandish promises our God sometimes reveals to us, but there is something in the spirit which witnesses 'this is of God'. And we need to move with that witness. In Abram's case, the Lord commanded him,

> *'Arise, walk in the land through its length and its width, for I give it to you.'* (Genesis 13:17)

And so, Abram *'moved his tent'* (Genesis 13:18), continuing his journey of faith with the Lord.

A time came when enemies took all who dwelt in Sodom captive, including Lot. An escapee informed Abram who immediately *'armed his three hundred and eighteen trained servants who were born in his own house, and went in pursuit'* (Genesis 14:14). In their pursuit, Abram and his servants were able to rescue all who came from Sodom and return them to their city with their possessions. The king of Sodom, who had previously fled the battlefield, went out to meet Abram in the King's Valley, and Melchizedek, king of Salem, the *'priest of God Most High'*, offered thanksgiving with bread and wine. Melchizedek is a type of Christ, being both king and priest, and being *'without father, without mother, without genealogy, having neither beginning of days nor end of life, but made like the Son of God, remains a priest continually'* (Hebrews 7:3). In this, perhaps, Abram could see the prophecy of the Word of God becoming God's own sacrifice in order to save us from our sins. Jesus Christ, our High Priest, does not need to sacrifice daily for sins, as other high priests, *'for this He did once for all when He offered up Himself'* (Hebrews 7:27).

Abram refused the king of Sodom's offer to take the possessions that they had recaptured from the enemy, saying,

> '... I have lifted my hand to the LORD, God Most High, the Possessor of heaven and earth, that I will take nothing, from a thread to a sandal strap, and that I will not take anything that is yours, lest you should say, "I have made Abram rich."'
> (Genesis 14:22-23)

If we compare this response to Abram's willingness to receive abundant wealth from Pharaoh, we may conclude that Abram is a man of contradiction. Yet, we need to realise that God will use incidents to bring blessings upon us, so that on other occasions we provide the blessings for others. To receive any financial gain would have been dishonouring to the Lord, and to his nephew Lot, suggesting that family loyalty is not reason enough to act.

On his return home, we find Abram troubled. When the Lord encouraged him, *'Do not be afraid, Abram. I am your shield, your exceedingly great reward'* (Genesis 15:1); Abram refered immediately to his greatest concern; *'Lord GOD, what will You give me, seeing I go childless?'* (Genesis 15:2). Abram, knowing God's protection and provision, shared frankly with the Lord *'Look, You have given me no offspring; indeed, one born in my house* [a servant] *is my heir!'* (Genesis 15:3). Abram had just rescued Lot, and returned him to Sodom. At least if Lot had remained in his home, Abram could have comforted himself in having a family member as heir to all that God had given him. However, instead it would be a servant, Eliezer the firstborn servant, who would benefit from all of Abram's accumulation of wealth. Abram was devastated, so much so that he repeated his accusation to the Lord a second time. Look and see how our God of mercy responded with no correction or admonishment, but instead, comforting words, *'This one shall not be your heir, but one who will come from your own body shall be your heir'* (Genesis 15:4). The Lord had previously promised Abram that his seed would be in number as the *'dust of the earth'*. It was at night as the two friends, God Almighty and mortal man spoke, and so the Lord led Abram out to view the night sky, and said,

> '... "Look now toward heaven, and count the stars if you are able to number them." And He said to him, "So shall your descendants be."'
> (Genesis 15:5).

God repeated a promise that He had already revealed to Abram, but this time the promise reached Abram's spirit for we are told,

Abram *'believed in the* LORD, *and He accounted it to him for righteousness'* (Genesis 15:6).

Our Lord God is both faithful and just, giving His children freewill. He did not demand that Abram would believe His promises, but rather chose to encourage him with the truth. The Lord knows our thoughts from afar. He understands our frailties and inability to receive His promises into our spirits. However, on His eternal calendar He has circled a date on which the truth will drop into our spirits. A promise that one day dropped into my spirit and transformed my life is that I am accepted by God when I have failed, as much as when I have done well, for Psalm 91:15 tells me that God hears me because I call to Him, and not just because I deserve to be heard. There will be times when we want to give up on God's promises, and other people may well choose to give up on us, but the Lord God Almighty has the full picture, and He will use the world around us to bring to life His promises for each of our lives.

Abram began to believe God's word to him that, even in old age, he would have a son. Yet, Abram found it difficult to receive the truth that the Lord would give the land of Canaan to him as an inheritance. He asked, *'Lord* GOD, *how shall I know that I will inherit it?'* (Genesis 15:8). Abram knew that God was promising the inheritance to his descendants, and that he would not see this promise fulfilled in his own lifetime. Unless the Lord granted him knowledge of the truth in his spirit, Abram would go to his grave uncertain. Our God is real with His people and He desires that His people should be real with Him. In order for Abram to receive the covenant security that he sought he should

> *'... Bring Me a three-year-old heifer, a three-year-old female goat, a three-year-old ram, a turtledove, and a young pigeon.'*
> (Genesis 15:9)

Abram laid them before the Lord and waited all day for Him to reveal His truth, but God seemed slow to act. Vultures swooped down, as on abandoned prey, but Abram drove them away, still trusting the Lord to fulfil His promises, for *'God is not a man, that He should lie'* (Numbers 23:19).

As the sun began to set, Abram fell into a deep sleep, *'and behold, horror and great darkness fell upon him'* (Genesis 15:12). The Lord revealed to Abram the future that was awaiting his descendants – their time of slavery in Egypt and their victorious deliverance, followed by their return journey to the Promised Land. However, Abram was to see none of this, for he was to go to his fathers in peace, dying at a *'good old age'* (Genesis 15:15). After the sun had gone down and it was dark, the Lord gave Abram a sign:

> *'... there appeared a smoking oven and a burning torch that passed between those pieces.'* (Genesis 15:17)

Had God completed the burning of the covenant sacrifice during the day it might be argued that it was the work of the desert sun. However, at night, unless a human could carry the torch, the work must surely have been the hand of God. Sometimes, we need such mighty signs to stand along side God's word to us, to bring us back to remembrance in our times of uncertainty. Today, such a sign could include getting an encouraging phone call on a phone that has been disconnected.

The Lord then made a covenant with Abram, setting out the boundaries of the Promised Land. God did not promise Abram, 'I will give to your descendants', but instead 'I have given.' God's promises are written in the heavenlies and will come to pass at the appointed time.

> *'Therefore, know that the LORD your God, He is God, the faithful God who keeps covenant and mercy for a thousand generations with those who love Him and keep His commandments.'*
> (Deuteronomy 7:9)

This incident reveals the close friendship that had developed between the Lord God and Abram – God's desires to share with Abram plans spanning over four hundred years, and Abram's desire and ability to hear not only God's voice but also His heart. God created humanity to be in communion with Him; He desires to share with each one of us His heart's desire for His chosen people. The covenant of God with sinners has always been by sacrifice and the shedding of blood. By sacrificing His own Son on the cross, who died for all men that we may be saved, all are invited into covenant relationship with the Father, and all can have a close friendship with God Almighty. And that is amazing, wonderful news! You and I are invited into the closest, most intimate relationship possible. Our God is not an austere governor demanding that we do 'A B C' in order to be accepted, but instead, He is a loving Father who desires to lead us as a shepherd leads his sheep along the right paths, leading us to safe and green pastures.

In Abram's life (after this revelation that he would become a father), everything in the natural remained unchanged; ten years after arriving in Canaan, Sarai being still barren came up with the 'perfect solution'. She asked Abram, *'Please, go into my maid; perhaps I shall obtain children by her'* (Genesis 16:2). And Abram obliged! We are not told in the Scriptures whether Abram had shared the Lord's revelation with Sarai, his wife. We know that Abram believed God; that He would give him a son, and the Lord accounted Abram's faith to him for righteousness. Yet, how quick we are to help God fulfil His plans – and get it wrong! How many times have I known in my own life, and the life of others, the same scenario? You've heard God speak a promise, but how can *you* make it happen? Maybe, just maybe, we need to change our approach to less speed, more meditation; a willingness to learn patience; letting go of the false responsibility that says we need to give credence to the Lord's promises. If the Lord said it, then the Lord will fulfil it! He promises,

> *'So shall My word be that goes forth from My mouth;*
> *It shall not return to Me void,*
> *But it shall accomplish what I please,*
> *And it shall prosper in the thing for which I sent it.'*
>
> (Isaiah 55:11)

Amen!

From this union Hagar, Sarai's maid, conceived a child and one hopes that 'all lived happily ever after'. Alas, no! Hagar, once pregnant, despised her mistress; and Sarai feeling shamed by this, put the blame on her husband. He, unwilling to get involved, gave Sarai permission to do with her maid as she wished. She chose to beat Hagar who consequently ran away.

> *'So the Angel of the* LORD *said to her, "Return to your mistress, and submit yourself under her hand."'* (Genesis 16:9)

The Angel of the Lord promised to multiply her descendants exceedingly, and so Hagar returned to Sarai. Abram, at the age of eighty-six, was at last a father, and named his son, Ishmael.

However, thirteen years passed before another significant event took place in Abram's life:

> 'When Abram was ninety-nine years old, the LORD appeared to Abram, and said to him, "I am Almighty God; walk before me and be blameless. And I will make My covenant between Me and you, and will multiply you exceedingly."'
> (Genesis 17:1–2)

Notice that with this promise comes a condition. How often do we want to take God's promises without fulfilling His conditions? Abram was told to walk before God and be blameless. For God to command Abram to be blameless, it had to be possible for him to succeed, as God does not allow any of us to be tested beyond our ability. If Abram, a mere man, could become blameless, then so can the rest of us. However, this is not to put shame or guilt on any of us for missing the mark, *'for all have sinned and fall short of the glory of God'* (Romans 3:23). The grace of God, not the determination of self, washes us clean from our sins, making us blameless:

> '... His divine power has given to us all things that pertain to life and godliness, through the knowledge of Him who called us by glory and virtue.'
> (2 Peter 1:3)

Within this conversation, the Lord changed Abram's name to Abraham, *'for I'*, said the Lord, *'have made you a father of many nations'* (Genesis 17:5). The Lord also changed Sarai's name to Sarah, promising to bless Abraham and Sarah with a son from her own womb, for *'she shall be a mother of nations; kings of people shall be from her'* (Genesis 17:16). Seeing as Abraham was now ninety-nine years old and Sarah, his wife, ninety years old, this suggestion could be considered a little far-fetched! Instinctively, Abraham laughed, and even suggested to God that He should transfer those unborn promises to Ishmael, a living son. Ishmael was now thirteen years old and, quite possibly throughout his life, Abraham had believed that the Lord was going to fulfil His promises through Ishmael. We too, can spend years misunderstanding God's promises to us. The Lord God responded with a very determined *'No!'* (Genesis 17:19), repeating His promise more strongly with the name and birth date of Sarah's child, Isaac. How blessed we are that when we attempt to dissuade God from blessing us, He does not become discouraged but more determined. What a gracious, faithful God we serve!

From this moment on, Abram needed to live his life as Abraham, a father of nations. In changing his name, the Lord was leading Abraham into a deeper revelation of who God was calling him to be. Abram's self-image had to change from a father of one son (and he born to a maid), to God's image of Abraham as a father of nations, and all before Isaac was conceived, let alone born. Abraham, then, had the responsibility of introducing himself afresh to family, friends, and acquaintances. Such revelations can lead to misunderstanding and ridicule. This was therefore one of those harrowing moments that at one time or another we must all face, as we decide what is more important, God's word or man's thoughts.

As part of obeying God's voice Abraham was called to be circumcised, along with all his male family and servants, even foreigners abiding in his home. This was to be a sign of the covenant between Abraham and the Lord forever, and to all generations. Paul explains that it is not circumcision but faith that makes a person righteous, for years earlier, *'Abraham believed God, and it was accounted to him for righteousness'* (Romans 4:3). The circumcision was a sign of the righteousness that Abraham had already received in believing God. The act itself was not an indication of a relationship with God, for even the unbelievers in Abraham's household were circumcised. Paul makes clear that physical circumcision benefits nothing:

> *'but he is a Jew who is one inwardly, and circumcision is that of the heart, in the Spirit, and not in the letter; whose praise is not from men but from God.'* (Romans 2:29)

Shortly after this time, the Lord visited with Abraham again, also bringing two angels with Him. Disguised in human form, Abraham did not recognise the Lord, but he was quick to offer hospitality to the strangers passing by. The three 'men' were able to wash and rest before Abraham set a meal before them. The hospitality of Abraham's descendants can be experienced today, not only in Syria, but also throughout Africa. The writer of Hebrews encourages us all:

> *'Do not forget to entertain strangers, for by so doing some have unwittingly entertained angels.'* (Hebrews 13:2)

Abraham entertained the Son of God, who is the Angel of the Lord (Genesis 18:13). We, in the 21st century western world, often excuse not giving sacrificially because we're too busy, yet it becomes our loss as the Lord promises us,

> 'Behold, I stand at the door and knock. If anyone hears My voice and opens the door, I will come in to him and dine with him, and he with Me.' (Revelation 3:20)

Anyone entertaining the Lord for dinner will surely receive much more than they give, as we find with Abraham and Sarah.

The Lord asked Abraham where Sarah was; the answer came, *'Here, in the tent'* (Genesis 18:9). The Lord knew where Sarah was, but wanted Abraham and Sarah to know that God intended Sarah to hear the conversation. And so, with audience in place, the Lord repeated His promise to Abraham,

> '... I will certainly return to you according to the time of life, and behold, Sarah your wife shall have a son ... ' (Genesis 18:10)

Sarah immediately laughed within. The Lord our God, who knows our innermost thoughts, asked Abraham why Sarah laughed. In fear, Sarah quickly denied laughing, but the Lord corrected her, *'No, but you did laugh'* (Genesis 18:15). This incident reveals two things: that Abraham, although having come to a place of believing God that He would give him a son by his wife, had not shared this revelation with Sarah; and secondly, that our thoughts cannot be hid from God, no matter how private we attempt to keep them. The Lord did not correct Sarah for laughing, but rather for lying. Our God would have us to be in truth, no matter how afraid we may be of the consequences! Abraham already believed God, yet God knows our need for an occasional 'top-up' in the faith department. This is why people receive prophecy after prophecy from different sources saying exactly the same thing. I once made a card with bluebells on it for a lady. Unbeknown to me she was praying for confirmation to stay with the vision that God had given her, and along came my card full of bluebells, a symbol of confirmation between her and the Lord.

As the Lord was leaving Abraham, He chose to share His plan to destroy Sodom and Gomorrah, the dwelling place of Abraham's nephew, Lot. Scripture tells us *'The secret of the* LORD *is with those who fear Him'* (Psalm 25:14). The Lord further substantiated this in the professing of Abraham:

> *'For I have known him, in order that he may command his children and his household after him, that they keep the way of the* L<small>ORD</small>*, to do righteousness and justice, that the* L<small>ORD</small> *may bring to Abraham what He has spoken to him.'*   (Genesis 18:19)

Let us look individually at the revelations that God's word unveils.

Abraham was to become a great and mighty nation

Sodom was the largest of five cities in a rich and successful nation, yet the people living there were about to be wiped out. Should this not serve as a warning to any person, group, or nation hoping to realise the dream or vision of becoming great and mighty, even in the work of the Lord? Good works cannot save us, but defying godly order can destroy us. When we forget God or, as with the Sodomites, never knew Him, then selfish pleasure and glory easily ensnares us.

All the nations of the earth are to be blessed in Abraham

We can see this was a prophetic word; Jews and Muslims see Abraham as the father of their faith, while all who choose to follow Christ are grafted into the family of God:

> *'For you are all sons of God through faith in Christ Jesus ... And if you are Christ's, then you are Abraham's seed, and heirs according to the promise.'*   (Galatians 3:26, 29)

Not only was this a prophecy, but it was also an invitation for Abraham to intercede on behalf of this perverted nation. If they were to be blessed and to be saved, it would be through Abraham.

And so, Abraham *'stood before the* L<small>ORD</small>*'* and asked, *'Would You also destroy the righteous with the wicked?'* (Genesis 18:22–23). Abraham knew God's character; he knew Him to be a just judge, and so appealed to His 'better judgment' declaring,

> *'Far be it from You to do such a thing as this, to slay the righteous with the wicked, so that the righteous should be as the wicked; far be it from You! Shall not the Judge of all the earth do right?'*
> (Genesis 18:25)

This is a fundamental key to successful intercession – to know the heart and character of God, and appeal to His nature, His faithfulness, His truth, His justice, His compassion, and His mercy. If you take on the heart of God, how could the God who owns that gracious heart possibly refuse you?

Abraham began his plea on behalf of the city by asking *'Suppose there were fifty righteous within the city; would You also destroy the place and not spare it for the fifty righteous that were in it?'* (Genesis 18:24). Abraham posed this question with powerful revelation – without the righteous upon the earth, the earth would be destroyed. Christians have a very important role to play in the salvation of those around us, not measured by the testimony of our lips, but by the testimony of the Holy Spirit dwelling within us. As Abraham continued to intercede for Sodom and Gomorrah, reducing the suggested number of righteous abiding there, he did so with humility; *'I who am but dust and ashes have taken it upon myself to speak to the Lord'* (Genesis 18:27). God allowing us to come close, to know His heart for the people, is no excuse for pride; God is still God, no matter how close He allows us to become!

Abraham's final suggestion of the number of righteous to be found in order to save the city was ten. Perhaps Abraham was confident that at least ten righteous people would be found, even in such a depraved place as Sodom. Alas, this was not the case. At most, one could suggest four righteous people were found; namely Lot, his wife and two daughters who were rescued while all the other inhabitants were destroyed. And yet, looking closer at this family we see that Lot's wife disobeyed God and was turned into a pillar of salt, whilst his daughters got Lot drunk in order to have him father their children. So possibly, there was only one righteous person in the whole city. He is referred to as *'righteous Lot'* (2 Peter 2:7), and yet Scripture tells us *'God remembered Abraham, and sent Lot out of the midst of the overthrow'* (Genesis 19:29). When you are concerned for your family's welfare, be encouraged by this scripture; our relationship with the Lord, and our heartcry for our kin, will bring about God's mercy towards them. What a wonderful testimony of God's faithfulness towards those who love Him!

The Lord reveals of Abraham, 'I have known him' *(Genesis 18:19)*
Because of knowing Abraham's character, the Lord was able to say that Abraham would command his children and his

household to keep the way of the Lord and perform righteousness and justice. If the Lord has known us, if we spend time with Him and we purpose to love His ways and follow His commands, then He will also be able to speak so confidently of our characters. Being known by God to do right in His sight also turns out to be the key to receiving God's promises over our lives, for the Lord concludes, *'that the L*ORD *may bring to Abraham what He has spoken to him'* (Genesis 18:19).

The following morning Abraham looked over towards Sodom and saw, in its place, the smoke of a furnace. What would our reaction be to this? Would we cry out to God that He hadn't been fair in asking us to intercede and then in not taking notice of our prayer? Or would we worry about Lot's fate? Abraham did neither of these things. Holding on to the truth that our God is faithful, he knew that God would not destroy the just with the unjust. Abraham could not see Lot with the physical eye, but in his spirit he would know that the Lord had rescued Lot. Abraham was able to trust his nephew to the Lord and move on, journeying south, setting up camp in Gerar.

For some reason, however, Abraham was still not able to trust his wife, or her beauty, to the Lord. Once again, Abraham chose to introduce Sarah as his sister, as even in old age she was beautiful enough to be requested by the king, Abimelech. This time the Lord intervened by threatening Abimelech in a dream; *'you are a dead man ... for she is a man's wife'* (Genesis 20:3), and commanded him to return Sarah to Abraham or face death. Not surprisingly, Abimelech called for Abraham and asked for an explanation for treating him so badly. Abraham responded, *'Because I thought, surely the fear of God is not in this place; and they will kill me on account of my wife'* (Genesis 20:11). Perhaps in Abraham's situation I'd react differently from the way I would hope, but my belief is that we should be able to travel to the most godless nation in the world (if the Lord directs us to do so), without ungodly fear or resolve, and with the fear and knowledge of the Lord sustaining us. As Abimelech restored Sarah to Abraham, he also gave him *'sheep, oxen, and male and female servants'* (Genesis 20:14). Again, Abraham left the situation richer than when he arrived, and this time even receiving money, as Abimelech gave him a thousand pieces of silver to vindicate Sarah (Genesis 20:16). God is gracious towards His chosen people, even when they do not deserve His gifts. In case you consider judging Abraham, remember God's commands, *'Do not touch My anointed'* (1 Chronicles 16:22), and *'who are you to judge another's servant'* (Romans 14:4), for God is at work!

When Abraham was one hundred years old, Sarah bore a son, just as the Lord had promised (Genesis 21:1). How's that for a centenary birthday gift! Abraham followed God's command in circumcising Isaac on the eighth day and, when Isaac was weaned, his father held a great feast. According to customs of native tribes today, this probably happened three to five years after Isaac's birth. On the day of the great feast, Sarah found Ishmael, the son of her servant Hagar, scoffing at Isaac, and insisted that Abraham *'cast out the bondwoman and her son; for the son of this bondwoman shall not be heir with my son'* (Genesis 21:10). Abraham was very upset and, obviously overjoyed to have received the 'son of promise' with his wife, recognised Ishmael as his son too! The Lord persuaded him to follow as Sarah requested, without concern for Ishmael's life, promising,

> *'Yet I will also make a nation of the son of the bondwoman, because he is your seed.'* (Genesis 21:13)

Note that purely because he was the son of Abraham, a faithful servant of God, Ishmael would be blessed. Can we not also claim such blessings for our children? Ishmael did not need to fulfil the conditions of the blessing because Abraham had already fulfilled them. The Lord said of Abraham that he would walk uprightly before God, commanding *'his children and his household after him, that they keep the way of the* Lord, *to do righteousness and justice'* (Genesis 18:19). If we want future generations to be blessed then we need to teach them the ways of the Lord, remembering that actions speak louder than words; which characteristics of God do we present in our relating to them and to others – family, neighbours, work colleagues, shop-assistants, even strangers? Are you willing to make a conscious decision to improve your practical training?

After Hagar and Ishmael's departure, time went by without any major events until the Lord commanded Abraham,

> *'... Take now your son, your only son Isaac, whom you love, and go to the land of Moriah, and offer him there as a burnt offering on one of the mountains of which I shall tell you.'*
> (Genesis 22:2)

Abraham responded speedily, embarking on a three-day journey with his son Isaac and two servants, until he recognised the place that God had purposed Abraham to sacrifice his son at. Take note that Abraham did not wait for a few days, hoping he had heard incorrectly, or even suggesting that given time the Lord would change His mind.

Abraham left the servants behind with the purposeful command,

> '... *Stay here with the donkey; the lad and I will go yonder and worship, and we will come back to you.*' (Genesis 22:5)

We do not need to share with people all that God has asked us to do. However, we can, by faith, speak out the expected results. Abraham was about to sacrifice Isaac, and yet was able to say, 'my son will return with me'. While Abraham was speaking on a natural level to his servants, his spirit was communicating with the Lord, saying 'I trust You'. When Isaac asked Abraham where the lamb for the sacrifice was, Abraham didn't falter in his reply, but responded, again by faith, *'God will provide for Himself the lamb for a burnt offering'* (Genesis 22:8).

Arriving at the appointed place of worship, Abraham built an altar, placed the wood upon it, and binding Isaac, laid his son upon the altar:

> '*And Abraham stretched out his hand and took the knife to slay his son. But the Angel of the* LORD *called to him from heaven and said, "Abraham, Abraham! ... Do not lay your hand on the lad, or do anything to him; for now I know that you fear God, since you have not withheld your son, your only son, from Me."*'
> (Genesis 22:10–12)

Turning, Abraham was able to see a ram caught in a thicket by his horns, and sacrificed this beast in the place of his son, Isaac.

Abraham was tested by the Lord and passed with flying colours! We might wonder how Abraham remained so calm in a time of such high demands from God, but he knew that the Lord had promised him, *'in Isaac your seed shall be called'* (Genesis 21:12). Abraham didn't know exactly what God would do and he didn't know that the Lord would intervene before Abraham's knife would take Isaac's life. However, he did know that God would be faithful to His word, *'concluding that God was able to raise him [Isaac] up, even from the dead'* (Hebrews 11:19).

So, why did the Lord test Abraham's faith? This exercise cannot have been for God's benefit, as many years earlier He affirmed in Abraham, *'I have known him'* (Genesis 18:19). The Lord already knew how Abraham would react, but can we be 100% sure of how we might react in a new situation? The practical benefit, therefore, had to be for Abraham and his son Isaac, learning with the greatest of certainty that the Lord was faithful and would always provide. A personal lesson to Abraham would have been regarding his own faithfulness to the Lord. The Angel of the Lord spoke to Abraham promising,

> *'... By Myself I have sworn, says the* LORD, *because you have done this thing, and have not withheld your son ... in blessing I will bless you ... because you have obeyed My voice.'*
> (Genesis 22:16, 17, 18)

In the past, the Lord based His promises on His knowledge of Abraham's character and the thought, 'I know he will do right'. Now, the Lord was saying, 'I have tested you, and you have done right in my sight.' The Lord's promises were still based on Abraham's character. The only difference was that Abraham was now able to see himself as God saw him.

There is such an abundance of gold within each believer, and the Lord desires us to appreciate it as much as He does. As gold needs to be refined to be truly appreciated, we also need experiences that will remove the impurities in our lives and enable us to uncover the beauty that is hidden. There are prophecies, both in the Old and New Testament, of Jesus' coming:

> *'... For He is like a refiner's fire ...*
> *He will purify the sons of Levi,*
> *And purge them as gold and silver,*
> *That they may offer to the* LORD
> *An offering in righteousness.'* (Malachi 3:2, 3)

A reason, therefore, for the Lord to purify our hearts through testing is that our offering may be in righteousness. The desired result is a deeper, truer relationship between God and man. The Lord says,

> '... *They will call on My name,*
> *And I will answer them.*
> *I will say, "This is My people";*
> *And each one will say,*
> *"The* L*ord* *is my God."* ' (Zechariah 13:9)

In the letter to the Corinthians, Paul spoke of the Day of Judgment, in which

> '*each one's work will become manifest; for the Day will declare it, because it will be revealed by fire; and the fire will test each one's work, of what sort it is.*' (1 Corinthians 3:13)

We are saved by grace. Nonetheless, our work will be tested by fire.

Abraham's obedience to the voice of the Lord was a work of faith, like precious gold, that could not be destroyed by fire:

> '*Was not Abraham our father justified by works when he offered Isaac his son on the altar? Do you see that faith was working together with his works, and by works faith was made perfect?*'
> (James 2:21–22)

We can thank God that He will never ask us to sacrifice another person's life, but He may ask us to sacrifice a relationship to Him. Indeed, He is likely to ask us to sacrifice to Him, the Refiner's Fire, every vision and every relationship it entails. Without refining, gold is not ready to be used by the goldsmith and we, likewise, are not prepared to be used by the Master goldsmith.

Like Abraham, if our vision is from God, the act of sacrifice should be relatively easy. Abraham believed God; that was an act of faith. But perhaps his reason for believing God was logic! It was logical for Abraham to believe that if, in obeying the Lord, he sacrificed Isaac, the Lord would then raise his son up again. According to the ancient historian Josephus, Isaac was twenty-five years old at the time that Abraham was ordered to sacrifice his life, and Ishmael was fourteen years older. For over forty years, then, the Lord had been building up Abraham's faith to believe God's confirmation, '*in Isaac your seed shall be called*' (Genesis 21:12). How could this word be true, except that God preserved his son's life? We can gain hope from Abraham's example and be as logical with the promises that God has made to us. And besides, if we're holding on to a false promise, aren't we better off sacrificing it to the Lord? We are always tested when we are asked to pray a prayer of sacrifice to the Lord, be it regarding relationships, job, home, or hopes and dreams. If we allow the Refiner's Fire to do His work in us, we'll emerge from the fire proven, ready for the next step!

Abraham's wife Sarah died when she was one hundred and twenty-seven years old. Abraham mourned and wept over her; for it's important to release our anguish. Then Abraham looked for a burial site to bury 'his dead'. As Abraham sought an appropriate burial site for, not only his wife, but also his family, he spoke with the local residents, the sons of Heth. With respect for Abraham, they offered to give the site he requested (Genesis 23:6). For Abraham, however, it was not enough to be allowed to bury his dead in another man's grave. Abraham offered the full asking price, receiving a legal document declaring Abraham owner of *'the field and the cave which was in it, and all the trees that were in the field, which were within all the surrounding borders'* (Genesis 23:17). We have seen in Abraham's life times when it had been right for him to receive wealth and possessions from others, as a blessing from the Lord. However, for the protection of his wife and future generations, Abraham needed to legally own the land in which his family was to be buried. If he was given the cave, the descendants of Ephron could then have claimed it back, claiming that Abraham had only been allowed to use it, rather than own it. Furthermore, if Abraham had only possessed the cave, then he and his descendants would have had to seek permission of the owner of the surrounding land to pass through the field. All of these things needed to be taken into account, for although our mortal lives are short, within those few decades we are held accountable for the blessings or curses that we pass on to future generations.

In his old age, we found that Abraham sent his most senior servant to his home country in order to find Isaac a wife. Abraham did not want a local woman to be Isaac's bride, who may have corrupted his morality, nor did he want Isaac to return to the land from which Abraham had come. The Lord had called Abraham to the land of Canaan for a purpose – to give it to the descendants of Abraham as an inheritance. Abraham, therefore, did not want Isaac, the son of promise, to move away from the land that God had chosen. Initially the servant was apprehensive. What if he could not find a virgin from Abraham's kin who was willing to return with him to Canaan? Abraham spiritually and emotionally released the servant by promising, *'then you will be released from this oath'* (Genesis 24:8).

The servant travelled with ten camels laden with precious gifts until he reached a city in the land of Mesopotamia. He then prayed to the Lord God of his master Abraham for success in his venture. Abraham had prophesied that an angel would direct the servant to the right woman. The servant, trusting Abraham's words, prayed to *'Lord God of my master'* (Genesis 24:12) for success in finding the right bride for Isaac. Before engaging in a personal relationship with Jesus people can see our faith in God and, like this servant, call out to our Lord God. The servant, standing by a well at the time when women came out to draw water, prayed for very clear direction:

> *'Now let it be that the young woman to whom I say "Please, let down your pitcher that I may drink," and she says, "Drink, and I will also give your camels a drink" – let her be the one whom You have appointed for Your servant Isaac."'* (Genesis 24:14)

Before the servant had even completed the prayer in his heart, he observed his request being fulfilled; Rebekah, the daughter of Abraham's brother Nahor, offered hospitality to the stranger, just as the servant requested of the Lord. Our God often answers our prayers before we express them, showing that He truly knows our thoughts afar off, and cares about each one of us, answering our individual prayers. It's exciting for a believer when Father God does this, but more so, surely, for a person on the brink of beginning a relationship with the Lord.

The servant was thrilled by the Lord's speedy response; he may have already believed in the existence of his master's God because of the fulfilment of blessings in Abraham's life, but here the servant experienced the Lord's provision firsthand. Firstly, he worshipped the Lord and then revealed God's direction to Rebekah. When he met the family, he was bursting at the seams with excitement, and insisted that he should tell his story before he ate. The following morning, when the family asked that Rebekah should remain a few days, the servant pleaded not to be hindered in a speedy return to his master (Genesis 24:56). As a believer, one is wonderfully privileged to receive news of another's first personal encounter with God. We may pray and share, and yet not be involved in the moment they received Christ. To be effective witnesses to God's glory, we must humbly admit that the Lord's provision does not depend on our involvement, but upon God's mercy.

Before dying at the age of one hundred and seventy-five years, Abraham married again. His bride, Keturah, bore Abraham six children. However, his eldest sons Isaac and Ishmael buried Abraham in the cave with his first wife, Sarah. Isaac and Ishmael were both to receive blessings because they were Abraham's sons. Even if in Abraham's lifetime it was not possible for them to be united, there was something special in the fact that Isaac and Ishmael honoured their father in burying him together. Abraham was a family man who loved both of his sons. At funerals, families often comment that the deceased would have appreciated the ceremony, and I'm sure Abraham would have appreciated this gesture from his two sons.

Practical application

We recognise in the story of Abraham that all promises have conditions attached. The recipients, as in the case of Isaac and Ishmael, need not necessarily meet the conditions as their father had already fulfilled the condition. So, what does this mean for us?

- ▶ Conditions are attached to the promises that God has made you. Just as a child who is unwilling to do their homework does not receive the treat promised by a parent, we will not receive God's promises unless we fulfil the condition. Facing a difficult situation, God may say to you, 'trust Me and everything will be ok.' His promise is to sort out your problem; the condition is that you trust Him. Or, if you want to overcome an addiction, the Lord may say, 'I'll set you free, but you must leave your old friends behind.' He promises to set you free from addiction, but the condition that you must meet is leaving old friends behind, and form new friendships in the body of Christ.
- ▶ We can provide a spiritual inheritance for our children by obeying the command of God in bringing up children in the way of the Lord.
    - Discipline yourselves to provide family worship time each day.

- Children love to have their parents' attention. Give them happy memories of spending time with God by being creative – teach them action songs, let them teach/act out the Bible stories, give them scripture (memory verses) to learn and recite, and encourage them with prizes (although judge effort, not perfection, so that all may excel).
- Relate the Bible teachings to the age of your children and to the world that they live in. Jesus' parables were full of objects familiar to the listener so give your lesson that extra edge by using objects to reinforce your point. When talking about Christians being the light of the world (Matthew 5:14), put a lamp under a coffee table, and ask, 'Does it give much light to the room?' and 'How can we make sure we are not hiding the light of Christ under a table?' The answer is by acting as Christ would. Children can think about sharing with others, whereas teenagers might think about saying 'no' to peer pressure to sin (Ephesians 5:1–14). One couple that I met found issues in the soap opera *Neighbours* a good opening for moral teaching.
- Reinforce your lesson in daily living. Don't forget what you have taught about cultivating patience when, for the umpteenth time, little Johnny is fighting with his sister! Find a way to discipline without losing your temper, forewarning your child of punishment, e.g. time out, lose a privilege, etc. However, *never* refuse love as a punishment; like our Father in heaven, your love must be unconditional.

Chapter 8
It's a Promise! Abraham and Sarah

Sarai was introduced as Abram's wife, but we later find out that she was also his half-sister (Genesis 20:12). Abram was seventy-five years old when the Lord called him out of his homeland to travel to the Promised Land. Sarah, nine years younger, was sixty-six years old. What an age to begin travelling! And, according to reports from the archaeologist C. Leonard Woolley who undertook extensive excavations in 1922–23 at Abram's hometown, Ur of the Chaldees, the couple, in choosing to travel, were giving up a high standard of living. A school was found in this excavation, and also homes of average middle-class families that had ten to twenty rooms, the lower floor for servants, and the upper floor for the family. Abram and Sarai therefore gave up the benefits of living in a highly civilised town in order to become nomads, dwelling in tents. Perhaps Sarai trusted Abram's judgment, or perhaps she had always hoped to travel. Perhaps though, as a wife, she had no choice!

Although Sarai was barren, the Lord had promised Abram, *'I will make you a great nation'* (Genesis 12:2). Abraham displayed wisdom in his response to this paradox, never once blaming his wife, but always relating his concern directly to the Lord, the Giver of Life. This could only prove to be beneficial for their marital relationship. Not every area of their relationship was as positive, however. Before long there was a famine in the land, and the Lord directed Abram to sojourn in Egypt. Even in old age, Sarai was beautiful, so much so that Abram was afraid the Egyptians would kill him in order to take her. As they neared Egypt, Abram asked Sarai, *'Please say you are my sister, that it may be well with me for your sake, and that I may live because of you'* (Genesis 12:13). Sarai dutifully obliged and sure enough, the princes of Egypt noticed her for her beauty and commended her to Pharaoh. Abram's opinion of Sarai's beauty was not simply the view of a bias husband – after all shouldn't every husband consider his wife beautiful! A description of Sarah on a scroll found in 1947 in a cave near the Dead Sea reads, 'Above all women she is lovely, and higher is her beauty than that of them all, and with her beauty there is much wisdom in her.'[2] Perhaps, in this final sentence, we are presented with the secret of Sarah's lasting beauty; true beauty comes from within, expressing the character and spirit of a person. Physical beauty usually fades with age, or at least becomes concealed behind the cracks and crannies of life! Beauty from within, however, if one will receive of God's wisdom, will increase with time:

> 'How much better it is to get wisdom than gold!'
> (Proverbs 16:16)

and

> 'She is a tree of life to those who take hold of her.'
> (Proverbs 3:18)

Sarai's beauty, though, created a problem for Abram. Sarai, introduced as Abram's sister, was taken into Pharaoh's home, with the intent that she should become his wife. Abram, having received the *mohar* (or 'bride price'), was treated very well for her sake, and was also given sheep, oxen, servants, donkeys, and camels (Genesis 12:15–16). Abram's manmade solutions, however, lost him his wife. But, the Lord, remaining faithful to his servant, resolved the problem. Pharaoh, being afflicted with many plagues, realised Abram's deception, corrected him, returned his wife to him, and then sent him away (Genesis 12:20).

So, did Abram learn from this experience? Did he realise that God was bigger than any situation, and that the He would not allow anyone to harm him, and no weapon formed against him would prosper? Not in this area, it seems! For later, when Abraham travelled to Gerar, he again introduced Sarah as his sister, allowing King Abimelech to take her into his home (Genesis 20:2). This time the Lord appeared to Abimelech in a dream to warn him from taking another man's wife. Not surprisingly, Abimelech was upset with Abraham. Nevertheless,

---

[2] *World's Bible Handbook*, Robert Boyd (Harvest House, 1991), p. 39.

he not only restored Sarah to Abraham, but also gave him animals and servants, as well as thirty pieces of silver in order to vindicate Sarah.

These occasions may have brought material wealth to Abraham and Sarah, but they also must have cost them dearly; I cannot believe that they continued their journey with the same sense of integrity. Fear of separation and abuse must have dominated Sarah's mind. As she was barren, did her sense of guilt and shame lead her to believe that she was not worthy to be protected and cherished as a wife? Why did Abraham not learn of God's protection over him, and feel the need to revert to a manmade plan of protection? Every time we become involved with lies, we chip away at our precious gift of integrity. Abraham may have excused himself thinking, 'I didn't really lie, she is my sister', but in reality, when he kept from the king the vital information that Sarah was also his wife, the consequences were the same as if he lied. Why then, do we seek manmade solutions in times of fear and uncertainty, protecting ourselves whatever the cost? I find in my own life that my mind works overtime, attempting to find a way out. This is before I make myself stop and lay it all down before God, sharing my anxieties with Him and then choosing to leave it with Him to sort out. And He always does!

Plenty of things happened in Abram and Sarai's life between these two incidents. Abram had fathered a child through Sarai's servant, and the Angel of the Lord had visited, promising that Sarah would bear a son *'according to the time of life'* (Genesis 18:10). At a time of uncertainty in Abram's life, he asked the Lord for a sign that He would bless him (Genesis 15:2). The Lord made a covenant with Abram to give him an heir from his own body. We are not told whether Abram shared with Sarai the promises that he had received from the Lord, but it is possible that Sarai's suggestion to Abram (to take Sarai's maid to birth a child on Sarai's lap) was a response to God's revelation. We very quickly see that this was man's interference, rather than God's direction. As soon as Sarai's maid became pregnant, she despised her mistress; this dishonour was too great for Sarai and as a result, she wanted Hagar dealt with accordingly. Abram's response was to wipe his hands clean of the problem; Hagar was Sarai's maid, not his! Abram's response was in accordance with their cultural beliefs; Sarai's maid was her responsibility, for her to do as she pleased, even if Hagar was carrying Abram's child. Once the child was born, however, Abram obviously formed a bond with his son, Ishmael, believing this was to be the child that God had promised (see Genesis 17:18–19). This may have been acceptable to Sarai when Ishmael was Abram's only son, but the time would come when things would be viewed differently.

In the meantime, God continued to pursue Abram with the revelation that a son would be born from Sarai's body. In accordance with the promise, the Lord changed the couple's names; Abram meaning 'High Father' was to become Abraham, 'Multitude of Nations', and Sarai, meaning 'Princess', was to become Sarah, 'Princess of a Multitude'. Abraham's initial reaction was to laugh – to suggest a one hundred-year-old man and a ninety-year-old woman could create a baby together may indeed be classed as foolishness, but the *'foolishness of God is wiser than* [the wisdom of] *men'* (1 Corinthians 1:25). The Lord, in being determined to bless Abraham, continued,

> *'But My covenant I will establish with Isaac, whom Sarah shall bear to you at this set time next year.'* (Genesis 17:21)

Furthermore, the Angel of the Lord visited in bodily form, assuring both Abraham and Sarah of this promise. Sarah's reaction, as her husband's before her, was also to laugh. This suggests that Abraham has not shared God's revelation with her prior to this occasion. When the Lord had spoken previously to Abraham, God's promise was within a very specific timescale, *'Sarah shall bear to you at this set time next year'* (Genesis 17:21). This promise also required a little cooperation from Abraham and Sarah to become a reality! For this reason the Angel of the Lord needed to repeat His promise in front of Sarah, assuring Abraham that Sarah would bear a son *'according to the time of life'* (Genesis 18:14). The promise of a child in old age was supernatural, but the process was to be natural; Sarah was to conceive a child and experience the time appointed for pregnancy. I know of many infertile couples that, having received prayer into the root cause of their infertility, have become parents nine months later, for the Lord is abundantly able to fulfil His promises to us (Romans 4:21).

Only a short time passed between this visitation and their travelling to Gerar. Is it possible that they hadn't yet joined together to consummate God's plan? Perhaps, as Abraham presented Sarah as his sister, Satan was attempting to utilise

Abraham's fear, encouraging him to separate from his wife so that the Lord's promise could not be fulfilled. However, our God has the immense skill, and the willingness of heart, to turn to good all that Satan means for evil (Genesis 50:20). There may be times in our lives when our own actions prevent us from walking in the promises of God. In these times of bad judgment, may the Lord do for us as He did for Abraham! Sarah, reunited with her husband, conceived and bore a son, Isaac, for *'the Lord did for Sarah as He had spoken'* (Genesis 21:1). The promises of the Lord towards us are always words of truth, no matter how bizarre they may appear; He is the God of impossibilities:

'For with God nothing will be impossible.' (Luke 1:37)

Sarah's response to bearing a son was to laugh. This was no longer the laughter of disbelief, as Sarah experienced great joy declaring, *'God has made me laugh, so that all who hear will laugh with me'* (Genesis 21:6). There are things so amazing in our lives that can only be the Lord's doing, that our reaction is laughter, a mixture of joy and astonishment. As motherhood brought a joyful sense of completion to her marriage, Sarah exclaimed, *'Who would have said to Abraham that Sarah would nurse children? For I have borne him a son in his old age'* (Genesis 21:7). This verse also confirms that Sarah's ninety-year-old body was given supernatural strength to follow the natural course of events – carrying a child in her womb, enduring the pains of labour, and producing milk to feed her child. Quite awesome, really!

We don't know how well Abraham's family adapted to their peculiar situation. Culturally, it was common for a husband to have more than one wife, and even to hire surrogate mothers, but it certainly wasn't common for a barren old woman to suddenly become fertile! Not only had Abraham believed for fourteen years that Ishmael was the heir that God had promised, but Sarah had probably resigned herself to this fact too. When Isaac was about four years old, and weaned from his mother's milk, Abraham arranged a great feast to celebrate the baby becoming a boy. Isaac was to be the centre of attention yet Sarah found Ishmael, now around eighteen years old, making fun of him. Perhaps Sarah had been feeling uncomfortable with Hagar and Ishmael's presence since the birth of Isaac. She, of course, was the person most responsible for Ishmael's birth. There must have been such regret in her heart. Ishmael scoffing at Isaac on his special day was probably the last straw. Afraid that Isaac's life would always be marred by this older boy's attitude, Sarah insisted that Abraham *'cast out this bondwoman and her son'* (Genesis 21:10). With contempt, Sarah no longer viewed them as surrogate mother and adopted child, but as slave and son. The conflict for Abraham was that Ishmael was still his son, 'flesh of his flesh', regardless of who the mother was. This conflict is widespread in today's society, with children of previous relationships not being accepted. The Lord told Abraham to comply with Sarah's wishes, which may seem a little harsh to us, but we must remember that Ishmael was a young man and therefore old enough to become independent.

The assurance that Isaac was the promised child would not have persuaded a loving father to let go of his older son; Abraham needed to hear that this arrangement would be best for Ishmael too. The Lord responded, *'I will also make a nation of the son of the bondwoman, because he is your seed'* (Genesis 21:13). There are some terribly difficult family decisions to be made in this nuclear age of one-parent families and rapid successions of stepparents. Hopefully, the majority of cases can see families coming to a place of peace in their new found relationships, although sometimes, like Abraham, the Lord would have us let go, although perhaps only for a season. Sarah was thinking of herself and her son when she insisted that Hagar and Ishmael be sent away, but the Lord wanted to use it for the good of all. Isaac needed to grow in a ridicule-free environment, while Ishmael needed affirmation for who he was, and not distain (from Sarah) for who he wasn't. By being forced out of his comfort zone, Ishmael called on the Lord, who *'was with the lad; and he grew and dwelt in the wilderness, and became an archer'* (Genesis 21:20). Later, we can presume that Abraham was reunited with his son Ishmael as he, alongside his brother Isaac, buried their father.

When the Lord challenged Abraham to sacrifice his son to Him, Abraham did not inform Sarah. Perhaps he considered that the burden of knowing was too great for Sarah. How would she rest while waiting for the return of her beloved son? Abraham's faith told him that even if he sacrificed his son's life, the Lord would raise him up again. Possibly, Sarah would reason that sacrificing Isaac would be putting the Lord to the test; therefore, it was best that she was not informed, rather than risk her attempting to dissuade Abraham from being obedient.

The next time we hear of Sarah is on her departure date,

having *'lived one hundred and twenty-seven years'* (Genesis 23:1). Abraham sought a burial place for Sarah, one that would become the family tomb. Over sixty years had passed since Abraham had last faced the issue of grief with the death of his father. Abraham grieved for the loss of his wife, crying over her. Perhaps, when someone dies young we grieve our loss of what could have been, given a little more time. In old age, the loss is no less, just different. We experience the pain of saying goodbye to those that we love, and we also bid farewell to a relationship that grew with time, and probably fitted 'like a glove'.

Personal application

As Abraham travelled through the Promised Land, depending on the promises of God, he proved to be a righteous man who was respected by his neighbours. However, each time he left the Promised Land his behaviour called his integrity into dispute. If we consider the Promised Land as our salvation, and the promises of God as that which we obtain when we remain in God's will for our lives, then we begin to see that we too lose our integrity when we visit 'Egypt' – the world's method of relating. Like Abraham, most of our Christian life/character is under the Lordship of Jesus, yet areas remain where we come out from under God's promises.

We need to:

- Make a conscious decision to bring this area under the Lordship of Jesus, allowing the Holy Spirit to reveal to us the root cause of our problem (Abraham's reason for transgressing the law of protecting his wife was due to fear).

- Release the root cause of the problem, repenting of taking it on, and forgiving anyone who may have been involved in transferring this wrong belief. Having witnessed my Mum receiving physical and mental abuse from her two husbands, I grew up with the wrong belief that all husbands hurt their wives, no matter how loving they are before marriage.

- Recognise ungodly vows that we consequently may have taken on, stopping us from receiving God's promises. Repent, and be forgiven. I, vowing to remain independent of others' help or love, blocked God's desire for me to be involved in godly relationships.

- Allow God to reveal His truth (*rhema* word) directly into our spirits. The power of the words, *'God has not given us a spirit of fear, but of power and of love and of a sound mind'* (2 Timothy 1:7), need to enter our spirits, to empower us to change our lifestyle.
- Walk in the new power of God's blessing over this area of our lives.

> *Lord,*
> *I allow You to be Lord of every area of my life. I repent of past disobedience to Your word, and for walking away from Your blessings. Please reveal to me the root cause of my sinful behaviour and release its hold over me. I forgive myself for taking on wrong beliefs and I also forgive others* [name them] *for being used by Satan to encourage me to believe in a lie. I repent of ungodly vows that I have made* [describe them] *and ask to be set free to enjoy the blessings. Please give me Your* rhema *word to empower me to walk in Your blessings in every area of my life. Amen.*

Chapter 9
Family Connections: Lot and the Lord

Lot is introduced to us as the nephew of Abraham (and son of Haran, who had died before the family left Ur of the Chaldeans). Initially, Lot's grandfather, Terah, took responsibility for Lot, but after Terah's death, Lot travelled with Abraham. When the Lord blessed Abraham with great wealth, He also blessed Lot, for the time came when *'the land was not able to support them, that they might dwell together, for their possessions were so great'* (Genesis 13:6). Contention grew between each of their herdsmen as a result of the lack of space. Abraham, not wanting to fall out with his nephew over this, *'for we are brethren'* (Genesis 13:8), suggested that they should divide the land between them, with Lot being given first choice. Lot was very swift to respond, allotting himself all the plain of Jordan, which was fertile land, well watered and pleasant to the eye. The author points out that this was how the plain looked before Sodom and Gomorrah were destroyed (Genesis 13:10).

This is the first glimpse we have of Lot's personality, and the view is unfavourable towards him. After being given first choice, Lot selected the best land and revealed his self-absorption. In choosing to reside in Sodom amongst people of disrepute, and for the sake of material wealth and success, Lot *'tormented his righteous soul from day to day by seeing and hearing their lawless deeds'* (2 Peter 2:8). He paid a high price to live in a fertile land! In time, a war broke out, and the inhabitants of Sodom, including Lot and his possessions, were captured. As soon as Abraham was informed of this, he and his trained army of servants went in pursuit in order to rescue Lot and his neighbours. Safely delivered from the hands of the enemy, Lot then chose to return to Sodom.

The next time we hear about Lot is when the Lord sent angels to destroy the city which had become Lot's home. As the angels (appearing as men) entered the city, Lot rose to meet them and offered hospitality, as his uncle Abraham had done before him. The men were content to sleep in the square, but Lot insisted very strongly that they should stay in his home. Only later in the evening, when from throughout the city men of every age demanded that Lot should hand over the strangers to be sexually abused, do we realise why Lot almost forced the men to take shelter in his home (Genesis 19:8). Lot was surrounded by extreme licentiousness, yet his urgency to protect the strangers reveals that he had remained righteous.

As Lot endeavoured to protect the strangers, the residents responded, *'This one came in to stay here, and he keeps acting as a judge'* (Genesis 19:9). This reveals how Lot had disputed with the men of the city on previous occasions by trying to introduce moral standards. Sadly though, Lot felt a greater responsibility for two strangers than he did for his own family, as he offered his two virgin daughters to the crowd to do with as they pleased. One would not want to dwell on the horrific ordeal that the girls could have suffered had the strangers not been angels. The fact that Lot's daughters were virgins, however, meant that Lot so far had been able to protect his children in an extremely dangerous environment. Now, unable to protect himself, the crowd pressed against Lot, being absolutely determined to take the strangers. The angels blinded the men, pulled Lot into the house, and explained the Lord's plans to destroy the city. Lot was told to inform the extended family, *'But to his sons-in-law he seemed to be joking'* (Genesis 19:14).

When morning arrived, the angels urged Lot to hurry, *'lest you be consumed in the punishment of the city'* Genesis 19:15). However, Lot still lingered, so the angels took hold of his hand and his wife's, and also his two daughter's hands, with *'the LORD being merciful to him, and they brought him out and set him outside the city'* (Genesis 19:16). This scripture makes me consider how much we believers of today can behave like Lot, lingering when told to move quickly, and not wanting to leave what is familiar even though it is not beneficial to us. The severity of our choosing to linger in an ungodly environment, even when our own actions are godly, ring out in the words of the angels; should we remain, we will be consumed in its punishment. Thank God for our Lord's mercy! For, just as the Lord rescued righteous Lot, so too will he take us by the hand and deliver us out of that place of destruction.

Having rescued Lot, the angels told him to escape to the mountains. Lot, however, was afraid of evil and death in the mountains; this is one reason, perhaps, why Lot chose to endure the wickedness of Sodom. The angels agreed to Lot's suggestion of a compromise – that the smallest city of the region, Zoar, would not be destroyed and therefore Lot could sojourn there. Jesus tells us that *'on the day that Lot went out of Sodom it rained fire and brimstone from heaven and destroyed them all* [the inhabitants]*'* (Luke 17:29). This suggests that grace had saved the city while Lot was present. Then too, as Lot travelled towards Zoar, this small city received grace, escaping destruction (Genesis 19:21). We are informed that, *'his wife looked back behind him, and she became a pillar of salt'* (Genesis 19:26). It is not that she was curious to see what was happening and was destroyed for looking behind her shoulder, but rather, her heart remained in Sodom, and so she lingered behind the rest of the family. Jesus says, *'Remember Lot's wife'* (Luke 17:32), when teaching about personal accountability and when warning against the temptation to turn back from the salvation of Christ for the sake of material wealth and earthly pleasure.

It is highly likely that Lot's wife physically became *'a pillar of salt'*, rather than this being a metaphor. Archaeological excavations in Pompeii, Italy, show that when Mount Vesuvius erupted in AD 79, poisonous volcanic gas asphyxiated many of the sleeping residents in the city, and then covered Pompeii with twenty feet of volcanic ash. Archaeologists found these sleeping bodies perfectly preserved, retaining their physical form. The residents of Pompeii, like Lot's wife, had been changed into 'pillars of salt'. The valley of Siddim, in which Sodom lay, now accommodates the Dead Sea, whose water contains high levels of bitter salt. Scripture tells us that all that *'grew on the ground'* was also destroyed (Genesis 19:25), and from that day to this, no plants have been able to grow there because of the salt content. Not only the cities, but also the valley in which they lay, were rained upon with fire and brimstone. As Lot's wife lingered behind, the debris would have captured her.

Lot, perhaps, felt disorientated and fearful in Zoar, and so escaped to the mountains with his daughters. Wanting to continue their father's lineage, the daughters got Lot drunk on two consecutive nights, and performed incest with him. This is a very sad conclusion to the story of 'righteous Lot'. Even though Lot never became involved in the sins of Sodom, by remaining there he had exposed his family to lewdness; raised in a city where sexual depravity was the norm, the girls considered it appropriate to have sex with their father. Sooner or later, we must all face the consequences of ungodly decisions. Modern thinkers insist that our children should be exposed to different sexual orientations. If we follow that path, we'll lead future generations back to Sodom and Gomorrah, and the destruction that awaits us there. Our children do not need exposing to these kinds of 'truths', but instead need protecting from them!

Personal application

Lot and his family lingered when told to leave Sodom, gathering their most valued possessions. When the angels led them out of the city, Lot's wife still lingered after the lifestyle that Sodom offered her. Licentiousness is often excused as 'modern thinking'. Lot's wife probably disliked the sinful environment she lived in, but enjoyed the benefits of an up-to-date city with all the latest merchandise available.

As our walk with Jesus deepens, He wants to purify our lifestyles more and more, and so we may find ourselves being led away from our comforts, perhaps through a fast. The most common type of fast is abstaining from food, but it needn't be so. The Lord showed me that I was emotionally dependent on chocolate and so, to break the dependency, He had me fast from chocolate. The withdrawal symptoms were excruciating, proving God's diagnosis. Are you willing to bring your personal fetish/comfort under the Lordship of Jesus by agreeing to fast from it for a set time? During the fast, allow God to teach you how to reverse ungodly responses into godly ones. Allow Him to show you the right level of involvement for you; can you enjoy 'creature comforts' without becoming dependent?

Chapter 10
The Quiet Man: Isaac and the Lord

Isaac was miraculously born to Abraham and Sarah in their old age. In birth, as in many events of life, Isaac typified the life of Christ – both births were announced and their names given by God, and both were born supernaturally; Jesus to a young virgin and Isaac to a barren woman past childbearing age. Although Abraham had another son, Isaac is referred to as his only son, the *'son of promise'* (Genesis 22:2), whilst Jesus is God's *'only begotten Son'* (John 3:16).

Little is shared in the Scriptures about Isaac's childhood, but there are numerous clues that reveal how his parents brought him up to honour the Lord as, *'Abraham circumcised his son, Isaac . . . as God had commanded him'* (Genesis 21:4). On a journey to sacrifice to the Lord, Isaac asked where the lamb was, showing that he was accustomed to this form of worship (Genesis 22:7). Later, we hear of him meditating (Genesis 24:63), and when his wife could not bear children, Isaac interceded on her behalf (Genesis 25:21).

One of the most famous stories in the Bible is the account of Abraham offering Isaac to the Lord. Again, we are able to see Isaac as a type for Jesus Christ. Jesus, of course, knew He was to be Father God's sacrifice, declaring, *'The Son of Man must suffer many things . . . and be killed'* (Luke 9:22), whereas Isaac went unknowingly to the altar (Genesis 22:7). Isaac carried the wood for the sacrifice (Genesis 22:6), while Jesus carried the cross on which he would be crucified (John 19:17). According to Josephus, the first-century AD Jewish historian, Isaac (aged twenty-five years) voluntarily submitted to his father's will, allowing Abraham to tie him up and lay him on the altar (Genesis 22:9). So too, Jesus, the Son of God, was willing to submit to His Father's command, laying down His life, declaring *'I am the good shepherd . . . and I lay down My life for the sheep'* (John 10:14, 15). God's intervention can be seen in both events – in Isaac's situation the Lord spoke from heaven, deterring Abraham from fulfilling the sacrifice of his son's life and provided a substitute in the form of *'a ram caught in a thicket by its horns'* (Genesis 22:13). In Jesus' case, God resurrected the 'sacrificial lamb' who had died for our sins (Acts 3:15).

Before Isaac's birth, the Lord told Abraham that the covenant that God had made with him would be established through Isaac (Genesis 17:21). For Abraham's lineage to continue, Isaac needed a wife. Not wanting his son to marry a local woman who might have practised foreign god worship, Abraham sent for a wife from his own kin when Isaac was forty years old. The servant's success in finding a wife for Isaac was swift because the Lord led him directly to Rebekah, granddaughter of Abraham's brother, Nahor. Although it was the duty of fathers to find a suitable partner for their children, we can clearly see that God our Father chose Rebekah as Isaac's wife.

> *'Now Isaac pleaded with the* LORD *for his wife, because she was barren; and the* LORD *granted his plea, and Rebekah his wife conceived* [twins] ... *Isaac was sixty years old when she bore them.'* (Genesis 25:21, 26)

Isaac obviously knew the power of persistent prayer, for the couple had been married for twenty years before they became parents. Isaac's requests did not diminish with time, but rather his request turned into pleading with the Lord. Having told Isaac about his own miraculous birth, and the timescale of events, his parents undoubtedly would have shared with their son the value of waiting on the Lord, for such times are designed to be periods of growth, as *'The Lord is not slack concerning His promise, as some count slackness, but is longsuffering towards us'* (2 Peter 3:9). Isaac remained confident in our faithful God, knowing that because of the Lord's mercy toward us, *'The effective, fervent prayer of a righteous man avails much'* (James 5:16).

Clara, a beautiful lady that I am privileged to know, rose at five-thirty each morning when her nine children were young to pray for their salvation. By the time they were in their teens all nine children knew the Lord, and now, as adults, each and every one of them is 'on fire' for the Lord. That's the power of persistent, sacrificial prayer!

Isaac and Rebekah's twins were named Jacob and Esau. In time, Isaac chose a favourite son, Esau, who was a successful hunter and a good cook. Perhaps favouritism felt perfectly normal to Isaac, having witnessed his brother, Ishmael, being sent away in order to favour Isaac as God's chosen heir. We can often taint the Lord's grace that is operating in our lives with our own prejudiced beliefs. We claim to be acting as God does, but because of our limitations, we become unfair and hurtful. Ishmael was sent away from Abraham, but not from the Lord. When the Lord appears to favour one person, He never abandons another, but fulfils His plans for each of them. Yet, when a father favours one child over another, he is rejecting the second child and creates unnecessary heartache and division. Father God always loves His children, nurturing, or admonishing, as the occasion arises; an earthly father needs to seek the Father heart of God for his own children, enabling him to be the representative authority that God has intended him to be.

In marriage, Isaac committed the same sin as his father had before him by pretending that Rebekah was his sister rather than his wife. There was a famine in the land, and just as Abraham had travelled to Gerar, so too did Isaac turn to the king of the Philistines for relief from hunger. The Lord directed Isaac to sojourn in the land, promising to bless him and perform the oaths that He had sworn to Abraham (Genesis 26:3–5). Isaac, like his father, could obey God's voice, but did not trust himself completely to the Lord's protection. When asked by the local men about his wife, he replied, *'She is my sister'* (Genesis 26:7), fearful that they might kill him for her if he admitted she was his wife. We may well have here the foundations for the popular sociologists' debate of 'nature or nurture?' As Isaac had not been born when Abraham deceived the Pharaoh of Egypt or the king of the Philistines, there is a suggestion that this behaviour may not have been learnt. If, on the other hand, we suggest Isaac's response is part of his nature, we excuse his behaviour, and therefore find a loophole for our own sinful behaviour. Bringing a spiritual dimension into the debate reveals that sinful traits that are not dealt with in one generation will be passed on to future generations through the law of curses and blessings (Deuteronomy 28). This does not give licence to sin, but rather brings awareness to the sins that we may be susceptible to, and need to guard against.

'All things are possible to him who believes' (Mark 9:23); therefore,

with the help of our Lord, we can overcome even the sins that have beset our families for generations. Bruce Wilkinson, in his book *Experiencing Spiritual Breakthroughs*,[3] records how he realised that when he was tempted to sin, he was actually seeking comfort. The promise of Jesus came into his memory,

> '... I will pray the Father, and he shall give you another Comforter, that he may abide with you for ever.'
>
> (John 14:16, AV)

As he prayed a prayer of desperation to be led away from sin by the comfort of the Holy Spirit, his request was answered. In subsequent times of temptation, Bruce testifies that the Holy Spirit always responds within three minutes, bringing him comfort and freeing his senses from the desire to sin. I too, have tried his 'three minute prayer' and found the Holy Spirit to be true to Jesus' promise.

Abraham's deception had been found out by revelation from the Lord. In Isaac's case, Abimelech looked out of his window *'and there was Isaac, showing endearment to Rebekah his wife'* (Genesis 26:8). As Abraham had been reprimanded for his behaviour, Isaac was corrected for opening the doorway of sin to the people of the land (Genesis 26:10). Yet, far from being exiled, Isaac came under the protection of the king, Abimelech, who charged the people saying, *'He who touches this man or his wife shall surely be put to death'* (Genesis 26:11). Without any sign of repentance, Isaac's sin was forgiven, and his debt to the Philistines remitted. Is our natural mind able to comprehend this result? Or must we look to the Spirit of Truth who will guide us into all truth (John 16:13)? Isaac, in many incidents, was a type for Christ, yet as a human with a fallen nature, was therefore susceptible to sin. Every story in the Bible leads to the cross of Jesus Christ if we allow ourselves to follow the trail; the covenant that the Lord made with Isaac rescued him from the debt of his sin, just as the new covenant that Jesus makes with us through the sacrifice of His blood sets us free from the debt of our sin. The Lord continues to turn situations around for us, even when we are totally to blame for any unpleasant, yet feasible, outcome. The same graceful God who remained loyal to His

---

[3] Wilkinson, Bruce and Kopp, David, *Experiencing Spiritual Breakthroughs* (Multnomah, 2002).

covenant to bless and multiply Isaac is ever faithful towards us also.

There's a further question of faith for Christians in Abimelech's response. Abimelech did not just forgive Isaac, but cancelled any due punishment for deceiving a king, and then also rewarded Isaac with royal protection. If he, a Philistine, was able to remit Isaac's debt, then shouldn't we hold a greater conviction to release people from the debt of sin against us? All of us need to work through the pain of being sinned against, and no one should remain in a dangerous relationship; however, the adage, 'we forgive, but we don't forget' seems a paradox to me, and finds a plausible argument in a statement such as, 'you once owed me £2,000'. Jesus Christ, the Son of God, shed His blood for us at Calvary, and proclaimed, *'It is finished!'* (John 19:30). As long as we choose to remember the debt, we deny that Christ has paid the price. In my experience, whenever I consciously remember a situation that's already been dealt with, I invite the spirit of unforgiveness to fight for ground that has already been won by the blood of the cross. Man naturally chooses not to forget a sin incurred against us, as a defence against further hurts, yet spiritually we are made in the image and likeness of our God and Father and therefore like Him, can choose to remember sins no more, forgiving a brother's sin up to *'seventy times seven'* (Matthew 18:22).

During his stay with the Philistines, Isaac proved himself a peaceful man.

> 'Then Isaac sowed in that land, and reaped in the same year a hundredfold; and the LORD blessed him.'   (Genesis 26:12)

As Isaac continued to prosper with flocks, herds and a great number of servants, the Philistines began to envy him, until it came to the point when Abimelech asked Isaac to leave the city; he declared *'you are much mightier than we'*, and so Isaac moved out to the valley (Genesis 26:16). There, finding disused wells that his father Abraham had dug, Isaac ordered his servants to re-open the wells; however, the local herdsmen claimed that the water was theirs. Instead of arguing, Isaac opened other wells, until he found one that was not disputed over. Isaac, being more powerful than the citizens of Gerar, could have fought for his rights, yet he preferred to seek peaceful solutions.

The persistent aggravation of people wanting to battle with

him drained Isaac, and so he travelled to Beersheba to hear the Lord's voice. Here, the late Abimelech had asked Abraham to vow on behalf of himself and his descendants to,

> '... not deal falsely with me, with my offspring, or with my posterity; but that according to the kindness that I have done to you, you will do to me and to the land in which you have dwelt.'
> (Genesis 21:23)

Isaac, it seems, was trying to be faithful to his father's promises, but the Philistines' jealousy towards him had become so demonstrative that living harmoniously with his neighbours appeared impossible. Isaac made the right decision to travel to Beersheba for,

> '... the LORD appeared to him the same night and said, "I am the God of your father Abraham; do not fear, for I am with you. I will bless you and multiply your descendants for My servant Abraham's sake."'
> (Genesis 26:24)

Only a short time later, possibly only hours, the Lord fulfilled His promises to Isaac in relations with the Philistines. Abimelech came out to meet with Isaac, but he responded, *'Why have you come to me, since you hate me and have sent me away from you?'* (Genesis 26:27). Isaac expressed his pain at being unjustly rejected by Abimelech and his people. Abimelech acknowledged that God had prospered Isaac to become great, and just as Abraham before him had been asked to make a vow not to hurt the people, the same request was made to Isaac. Furthermore, Abimelech prophesied, *'You are now the blessed of the LORD'* (Genesis 26:29). See how the Lord God will use even pagans to confirm his promises towards us.

> 'Then they arose early in the morning and swore an oath with one another; and Isaac sent them away, and they departed from him in peace.'
> (Genesis 26:31)

Isaac, the peacemaker, reaped the benefit of a godly attitude, and was left to dwell in peace.

When Isaac believed he was dying he called for his eldest son in order to bless him with the blessing that was reserved for the firstborn. However, while Esau was hunting game to prepare a meal for his father, Jacob disguised himself as his elder brother to enable him to steal the blessing. The realisation of what his younger son had done was a painful blow to Isaac; distressed over Jacob's deception, Isaac probably grieved the loss of any respect that he had hoped his son held for him. Yet, Isaac did not wipe his hands of his deceitful son, as so many hurting fathers are tempted to do. Instead, when Rebekah requested that Isaac send Jacob to her brother to find a wife, Isaac released him, blessing his son again. This time Isaac blessed Jacob in his own right, a blessing even fuller than the one he had obtained by deception, for Isaac prayed that Jacob would receive the blessing of Abraham (Genesis 28:3–4), demonstrating that Isaac recognised Jacob as the promised heir. How did this transformation come about? When Isaac was preparing to bless his son Esau, to be master over his brother Jacob, he either did not understand the Lord's plan, or chose not to understand. However, being shocked by Jacob's deceptive behaviour probably led the reflective Isaac into the presence of Almighty God to receive some important answers. Encouraged and comforted, Isaac could bless his son with revelation of the Lord's promises for Jacob and his descendants. However, a wise father chastises his son, and so even though he was rich and could spare any amount of animals, Isaac sent his son by foot to the land where he was to be trained directly by the Lord God to pick up the baton and run with the blessings of Abraham.

Isaac was a quiet, peaceful man who, although he lived on after sending Jacob away, was only mentioned again in relation to Jacob's return to the Promised Land. Isaac lived one hundred and eighty years.

> 'So Isaac breathed his last and died, and was gathered to his people, being old and full of days.' (Genesis 35:29)

Personal application

Isaac, born because of God's faithfulness, answered every problem with the same solution – persistent prayer. He trusted God to give him a son and heir and, when Jacob tricked him to give him the blessing of the firstborn, he was humble enough to bless him a second time, this time as the Lord's chosen heir. Grace from God's presence alone enables us to respond against 'human nature'. A couple I once lived with turned against me without reason. The Lord, protecting me from offence, graced me to respond with love and blessings.

How do we cultivate a life of persistent prayer? Ronald Dunn suggests some pointers in his book *Don't Just Stand There, Pray Something!*[4]

- ▶ While some people say it's wrong to keep 'pestering' God, Jesus teaches to pray persistently until we get an answer (Luke 11:5–13; 18:1–8).
- ▶ God will confirm His will to us through peace ruling in our hearts (Colossians 3:15):
  - Our spirits will know the outcome before it happens in the natural; in being assured that God is saying 'yes' to our request, our pleading turns to thanksgiving.
  - When God is saying 'no', our spirits witness a restraint to pray into that area. A friend was once praying for an ill person to recover. The Lord steered her to pray for a peaceful death, until she witnessed in her spirit that the man had gone to be with the Lord. A phone call later confirmed this.

---

[4] Dunn, Roland, *Don't Just Stand There, Pray Something!: Discover the Incredible Power of Intercessory Prayer* (Zondervan, 2001).

Chapter 11
Meant to Be: Isaac and Rebekah

Isaac was forty years old when he married Rebekah. In marriage, as in many incidents of life, Isaac typified our Lord Jesus Christ. A servant was sent to find a bride for Isaac (Genesis 24), just as the Holy Spirit finds a bride (the Church) for Jesus. As the servant spoke in the authority of Abraham, the Holy Spirit speaks in the authority of the Father. Rebekah, willing to receive a husband she had never met, typifies the Church receiving Christ; *'whom having not seen, you love'* (1 Peter 1:8). Isaac, in going out to meet Rebekah as she arrived, symbolises Christ coming for His bride,

> *'For the Lord Himself will descend from heaven with a shout ... Then we ... shall ... meet the Lord in the air ... '*
> (1 Thessalonians 4:16, 17)

Paul, the author of the Thessalonians, continues *'comfort one another with these words* (1 Thessalonians 4:18). Interestingly, Isaac was comforted by Rebekah's presence three years *'after his mother's death'* (Genesis 24:67). Although there is a general grieving cycle, grieving is as unique as the relationship that has been lost. Life is full of change; joyful changes, such as a new job, home or relationship, and the painful changes of letting go of the old lifestyle and the relationships it held. The lengths of time that individuals need to adapt to changes in life vary. In Isaac's situation, we can see the grace of God in action; had Rebekah been sent any earlier, Isaac, not yet ready for an intimate relationship, may have resented Rebekah's presence. The Lord knows our deepest needs, and brings us into new relationships when they will be most beneficial. Isaac *'took Rebekah and she became his wife, and he loved her'* (Genesis 24:67), again typifying

Christ, in that He *'loved the church and gave Himself for her'* (Ephesians 5:25).

Rebekah came into the marriage with a blessing from her family; *'may you become the mother of thousands of ten thousands'* (Genesis 24:60). These words proved to be prophetic, although Rebekah did not naturally conceive. Isaac, undeterred, went directly to the Lord, pleading for the healing of Rebekah's womb. The couple waited twenty years for the fulfilment of God's promise to Abraham that, *'in Isaac your seed shall be called'* (Genesis 21:12). Whatever your situation is that calls you to a place of faith, if you know that God has said it, then you know He will fulfil it. Amen!

When Rebekah conceived twins, the children struggled together within the womb. Rebekah, although knowing that the pregnancy was the work of the Lord, was concerned about the movement within her, and went to inquire of the Lord:

'And the LORD said to her,

'Two nations are in your womb,
Two peoples shall be separated from your body;
One people shall be stronger than the other,
And the older shall serve the younger."' (Genesis 25:23)

These days, without a scan, we cannot be certain that a mother is carrying twins, and yet thousands of years ago a shepherd's wife heard God tell her she was to bear twins. Rebekah obviously had a close relationship with the Lord. This is the first recording since the fall, of a married couple that related directly with the Lord. This had to be the perfect match (although not the perfect marriage, as there's no such thing!)

'So when her days were fulfilled for her to give birth, indeed there were twins in her womb.' (Genesis 25:24)

The boys were very different; the first, Esau, was red and hairy, destined to become a skilful hunter and a man of the field; the second, Jacob, was smoother skinned, and a mild man who preferred to dwell in tents.

'And Isaac loved Esau because he ate of his game, but Rebekah loved Jacob.' (Genesis 25:28)

Isaac appears to have been more like Jacob, a mild and reflective man, yet he preferred Esau to his younger son. Maybe it was a case of opposites attract. Perhaps Esau resembled Isaac's wife (his mother) in temperament. Scripture only tells us that Isaac loved Esau because he enjoyed eating his game, giving weight to the proverb 'the way to a man's heart is through his stomach'! Meanwhile, Rebekah loved Jacob, presumably because of the revelation that she had received from the Lord.

It's very sad to read of favouritism in the Patriarch family, as it can encourage division and competitiveness. Consider it a warning, rather than an example to follow! An example of godly parenting that should be emulated might be more readily found in the mother of John and Charles Wesley, the founder of the Methodist Church and the well-known hymn writer, respectively. Of her ten children, these two boys were to become famous Christians, yet Susanna Wesley gave individual Bible study and prayer time to each of her children. Every person has a special calling on his life, and some become predominant figures in the world arena, whereas others witness in their own small neighbourhood. However, all remain equal in the Lord's eyes. Parents, you are your children's first teachers, and you have a responsibility to direct a child into a relationship with the Lord, and to help them find their own special place in God's plan. Isaac allowed his natural appetite to direct his affections, while Rebekah abused God's words to excuse favouritism. Children are a blessing from the Lord, no matter what their personality or calling, and should therefore be treated as such!

The consequences of favouritism came to a head when Isaac, believing that he was near to death, called Esau to give him the blessing of the firstborn son. While Esau was sent to hunt and prepare a meal for his father, Rebekah directed her favourite son, Jacob, in a cunning plan to deceive his father and 'rob' Esau of his birthright. Rebekah, believing that the Lord had promised the blessing of the firstborn son to Jacob, and like her mother-in-law before her, erroneously saw it as her responsibility to bring God's promises to fruition. When Jacob feared the consequences of being found out, Rebekah replied *'Let your curse be on me, my son; only obey my voice'* (Genesis 27:13). As Isaac was now blind, Rebekah concentrated on making Jacob smell and feel like Esau, dressing him in Esau's best clothes and covering his neck and arms with goatskins.

No sooner had Jacob received the blessing and left Isaac's tent, than Esau arrived. Realising what Jacob had done, both father and son were grieved by Jacob's deceptive act, but no mention was made of Rebekah's sin. Esau swore to kill his brother after the days of mourning for his father, and so Rebekah persuaded Isaac to send Jacob to safety, to her own kin. She made no mention of Jacob needing to flee for his life, but rather directed her husband's attention to Jacob needing to find a good wife. Isaac may well have been 'the head of the household', but Rebekah, well versed in presenting a good case, often behaved as the 'neck' that moved the head!

So, what curse did Rebekah bring on herself for her son? When Rebekah sent Jacob away, she asked him to stay with her brother for a few days *'until your brother's anger turn away from you ... then I will send and bring you from there'* (Genesis 27:45). Rebekah was obviously a 'fix-it' kind of person, but this time things weren't so simple as she never sent for her favourite son. In the twenty years that Jacob was away, Isaac remained alive, and Esau presumably never let go of his bitterness and resentment towards Jacob. Rebekah's curse, then, was the bereavement of her favoured son who, though alive, would never live in closeness with his mother again.

If Isaac's life is chronologically recorded in Genesis, we can then presume that sometime between the twins' birth and their fortieth birthday, Isaac and the family moved to Gerar, to sojourn while there was a famine in the land (Genesis 26:1, 34). Isaac committed the same sin against his wife as his father Abraham had done against his mother, in presenting her as his sister in order to protect his own life. Rebekah's situation was different to Sarah's; she was a mother, and so in a society where barrenness was seen as a curse, she would have possessed a higher self-esteem than Sarah. She also remained in the family home, not experiencing abandonment and loneliness as Sarah may have done. In fact, Rebekah may have felt very secure in her relationship with her husband, with the king realising their true relationship when he saw Isaac showing endearment to his wife. Isaac and Rebekah were possibly married for fifty or sixty years by this time, and yet the love that Isaac felt for his bride had not faded over time (even if he was cowardly and presented her as his sister!)

Although Rebekah's departure from this world is not recorded in the book of Genesis, we know that she was buried with her husband, parents-in-law and favourite son, Jacob (Genesis

49:31). In death, as in life, Rebekah was close to the two people – Isaac and Jacob – who mattered most to her.

Personal application

During their early years, Isaac and Rebekah showed great potential for a godly marriage, as both had strong relationships with the Lord. Isaac spent time meditating (Genesis 24:63) and was a persistent intercessor (Genesis 25:21), whilst Rebekah heard the Lord's voice (Genesis 25:22–23). Yet, the one thing that should have cemented their relationship more than anything else – when they became parents together – created division instead. Each favouring one child over the other created two teams in the family instead of one united front. Parents who desire a peaceful family life cannot afford to favour one child above another. All children need to be loved and cherished to grow into healthy, well-adjusted adults. One sign of our fairness in relating to children within the family is the prayers that we pray for them. In committing to pray for our children with God's word rather than human judgment, we then begin to see our children and their lives as God sees them.

> *Dear Father,*
> *We thank You for our children whom You have given to us as a heritage and reward. We speak Your blessing over their lives. Children, may you worship God in spirit and in truth, with God energizing and creating in you the power and desire to work for His good pleasure. May you attend to His words, consenting and submitting to His sayings. Keep them in the centre of your heart, for they are life to those who find them, healing and health to all their flesh. Let your lives lovingly express truth. May your tongue be like the pen of a ready writer, graciousness pouring forth from your lips, mercy and truth written upon your heart. Enfolded in love, may you grow up in every way into Christ, the Head of the Church.*
>
> *Children, you are God's own handiwork. May you live your lives according to His excellent plans for you, taking the paths that He has prepared for you. May your work be honourable, earning a living with your own hands. If the* Lord *wills for you to marry, may you and your spouse esteem and delight in one another, bearing children who revere the* Lord*. May you prosper and be in good health, even as your soul prospers. For I know the*

thoughts that I think towards you, says the LORD, *thoughts of peace and not of evil, to give you a future and a hope. Amen!*

(Unless otherwise stated, this prayer was formed from the Amplified Bible: Psalm 127:3; John 4:23; Philippians 2:13; Proverbs 4:20–22; Psalm 45:1–2; Proverbs 3:3; Ephesians 4:15; 2:10; 1 Thessalonians 4:11–12; Psalm 128:3; Ephesians 5:2; 3 John 2; Jeremiah 29:11, NKJV.)

Chapter 12
Building Trust: Jacob and the Lord

Jacob, the second twin born to Isaac and Rebekah, was chosen by God to be a nation, stronger than his older brother (Genesis 25:23). Even at birth, this second son took hold of Esau's heal, which is why he was given the name Jacob, meaning 'supplanter' – one who replaces, displaces, ousts, supersedes or takes the place of another. Jacob further earned the right to the name in insisting that his hungry brother should sell his birthright to him, in exchange for some stew, and he also earned it when he disguised himself as Esau in order to receive the blessing of the firstborn from his father (Genesis 27). Esau, as one can imagine, was furious and vowed to kill his brother. Their mother, Rebekah, stepped in and had Isaac send Jacob to Rebekah's family. With the natural eye, it would appear that Jacob was moving away from the blessings claimed on his life. Far from being master over Esau, Jacob was 'run out of town' by his big brother.

Jacob made a big mistake in trying to achieve spiritual blessings with fleshly scheming. Such plans are impossible to achieve, but God will allow us the process and the consequences of our mistakes so that we may learn and grow from the experience. Up until this point, there is no suggestion that Jacob had ever had a personal encounter with God. On his journey, Jacob found himself alone, forced out of his place of comfort and security. This very insecure time for Jacob proved to be a wonderful opportunity for God! No longer full of his own ability, Jacob was now ready to hear God's personal promise to him.

As Jacob slept, he dreamt of a ladder upon the earth reaching to heaven, with the angels of God ascending and descending:

> 'And behold, the LORD stood above it and said: "I am the LORD God of Abraham your father, and the God of Isaac; the land on which you lie I will give to you and your descendants . . . Behold, I

am with you and will keep you wherever you go, and will bring you back to this land; for I will not leave you until I have done what I have spoken to you."' (Genesis 28:13, 15)

Let us look at this amazing encounter little by little. The angels ascending and descending the ladder between heaven and earth represents God's constant relationship with, and protection over, those who call out to Him. Having deceived his earthly father (Genesis 27:12), Jacob may have considered himself unworthy to even be recognised by God, but here the Lord showed Jacob that He chose to relate to him. Just as He was the Lord God of Abraham and Isaac, He was also willing to be Jacob's God through a personal relationship. Jacob was probably fearful of Esau's threats, but the Lord promised to protect him. Jacob had a long journey ahead of him to a strange land and our Lord promised to be with him. Jacob had also become an exile, yet our Lord promised to bring him back. Furthermore, as a guarantee, the Lord God saw it fit to promise Jacob that He would not leave him until His word was fulfilled.

When our Lord speaks so strongly to you, especially at a time when 'natural' optimism is drained from you, then you know that God has spoken His word to you! On one occasion, when my Mum had a major stroke in hospital, I was called home from London. Before my journey, I was frantic with worry, but as I travelled my spirit was calmed more and more by the presence of the Holy Spirit; I almost floated into the hospital and was not the least bit phased by Mum's condition! That night, in a dream, I saw the family preparing a party to celebrate our mother's healing. When I woke, I knew that dream was from the Lord, and when I rang the hospital, the nurse shared how amazed the staff were to have seen my Mum recover so much in the night.

Meanwhile, Jacob, assured of God's promises, continued his journey to his uncle's house. Laban had two daughters, Leah, the elder, and Rachel, whom Jacob loved. Jacob offered to serve Laban for seven years in exchange for marrying Rachel, only to be deceived by Laban into receiving Leah as his wife. After his initial upset, Jacob agreed to Laban's offer of Rachel, 'on credit', in exchange for another seven years working. We never hear Jacob complaining at not having received a tangible wage. Indeed, when the time was up, he was quite willing to return to his homeland with nothing more than his wives and children. God's plan, however, was to bless him greatly.

When Jacob requested Laban's permission to leave, Laban asked him to stay. He acknowledged God's blessing upon him since Jacob's arrival, and gave his son-in-law the right to name his wage. Jacob agreed,

> 'For what you had before I came was little, and it has increased to a great amount; the LORD has blessed you since my coming ...'
> (Genesis 30:30)

Through this bold statement, we recognise that Jacob believed God's word to him. During the years in which Laban's wealth increased, yet Jacob received no material wealth, Jacob could so easily have adopted the attitude of jealousy and self-pity. Instead, he sees God's blessing upon Laban as a direct result of his own presence. That's what I call confidence! Jacob was confident in His relationship with the Lord and the promises that his God gave to him; that He would bless those who blessed Jacob. Jacob had made two seven-year agreements with Laban, to work in exchange for Laban's daughters, during which time he would have also received food and lodgings. We can so easily make an agreement with another, and then become resentful when we appear to be receiving the short end of the stick. Jacob, however, continued to faithfully attend to the work that he had agreed to do, and even was able to see God's hand at work.

I find it very interesting that Jacob was willing to return to his homeland with nothing more than his wives and children. Children are an inheritance, and sons were especially seen as great wealth to the Israelites. Yet, from having Irish immigrant parents, I know firsthand the compelling desire to at least appear wealthy and successful when returning home. What strength of character Jacob must have had to remain confident in God's promises, willingly returning without material wealth. Fourteen years earlier, when the Lord appeared to him, Jacob made a vow:

> '... If God will be with me, and keep me in this way that I am going, and give me bread to eat and clothing to put on, so that I come back to my father's house in peace, then the LORD shall be my God.'
> (Genesis 28:20–21)

So far, God had fulfilled all of Jacob's requirements. Jacob did not ask for great riches in a foreign land, but for peace so that he could return to his father's home – a much greater gift than any amount of wealth could purchase. Jacob did not attempt to become rich working for his uncle, but the Lord planned it anyway!

When beginning a new contract with Laban, Jacob initially asked for the spotted and speckled sheep and goats, and the brown lambs. The herds were divided, with Jacob continuing to shepherd both flocks. The Lord blessed Jacob who *'became exceedingly prosperous, and had large flocks, female and male servants, and camels and donkeys'* (Genesis 30:43). We have evidence of God's plan to bless Jacob, in that while Laban changed Jacob's wages ten times, whatever colour or pattern animals that Laban chose for Jacob's wage, all the flock would bear such (Genesis 31:7–9). This constant changing of the rules, however, would have been unsettling for Jacob. Although he served Laban with all his might (Genesis 31:6), he could never please him, whilst Jacob's brothers-in-law becoming increasingly bitter towards him (Genesis 31:1). Jacob pursued the same principle that Paul the apostle had encouraged the Thessalonians to follow,

> *'See that no one renders evil for evil to anyone, but always pursue what is good both for yourselves and for all.'*
> (1 Thessalonians 5:15)

However, Jacob was unable to win peace with his in-laws. It was time then for the Lord to speak: *'Return to the land of your fathers and to your family, and I will be with you'* (Genesis 31:3). If we want to know when to go and when to stay, then we need to be listening to God. Jacob was probably fed up with Laban's deception long before he changed his wage for the tenth time, but if he had packed his bags earlier, he would have been guided by his own emotions rather than by the voice of God.

Jacob, in explaining to his wives that he planned to flee without warning Laban, shared both the natural reasons for leaving (problems with Laban), as well as the dream that the Lord had given to him that commanded Jacob to fulfil his vow to the Lord and return to his homeland (Genesis 31:13). Along with these instructions, the Lord had repeated his promise, *'and I will be with you'* (Genesis 31:3). This is key! Unless the Lord is with us, then our efforts are in vain (Psalm 127:1). We often cannot see the best solution with the natural eye; we need to hear the voice of God directing us, for His promise to those who place their trust in Him is:

> *'I will instruct you and teach you in the way you should go;
> I will guide you with My eye.'* (Psalm 32:8)

Jacob had a three-day lead before Laban was informed of Jacob's departure (Genesis 31:22). Laban pursued Jacob, determined to take back all that was his (in his mind everything, except Jacob, was his – daughters, grandchildren, flocks and servants) (Genesis 31:43). Unable to apprehend Jacob immediately, we see that God often uses time and circumstances to transform our hearts. After seven days travelling, Laban, knowing he was close on the heels of Jacob, perhaps fell to sleep, meditating on the action that he would take against Jacob as soon as he caught him. And the Lord spoke to Laban in a dream, *'Be careful that you speak to Jacob neither good nor bad'* (Genesis 31:24). The Lord had promised to be with Jacob. When God is with you, He protects you from harm and miraculously turns situations around. Laban adhered to the Lord's warning, and sought only an explanation from Jacob. Laban's yearning for revenge had turned to a desire for peace. Together, they built a heap of stones, with Laban announcing it

> *'... a witness, that I will not pass beyond this heap to you, and you will not pass beyond this heap and this pillar to me, for harm.'* (Genesis 31:52)

The Lord's blessing was in this event; Jacob needed to be at peace with his past, before pressing on into his future. The Lord allowed Laban to pursue Jacob, not to exact revenge, but to free Jacob completely.

It sometimes appears as if God clears away one set of problems only to then release us into the next set. No sooner had Laban's fury towards Jacob receded, then Jacob heard that his brother, Esau, who had vowed to kill him two decades earlier, was coming towards him, accompanied by four hundred men (Genesis 32:6). Jacob had hoped to appease Esau by sending gifts to him, but his response suggested that war, rather than peace, was on Esau's mind! Disturbed by this news, Jacob didn't find time to communicate with the Lord. Depending instead on human resolve, he divided his company into two, hoping that, at most, only half of his group would be taken. This deed done, Jacob then confessed to his Lord God,

> *'I am not worthy of the least of all the mercies and all the truth which You have shown Your servant; for I have crossed over this Jordan with my staff, and now I have become two companies.'*
> (Genesis 32:10)

The Lord had promised to bless and protect Jacob, and all who were with him. In attempting to preserve half the group, Jacob realised that he did not have complete faith in God's promises. Had Jacob not repented of his mistake, bringing him back under the Lord's protection, some misfortune may well have overtaken one of the groups. In response to our repentance, our God brings us back under His protection. Within Jacob's prayer, Jacob reminded God of His promises made to Jacob. This form of prayer is more for our benefit than the Lord's; He neither forgets nor relinquishes His promises to us. We, on the other hand, need to reawaken our confidence in God's promises when a situation appears to be hopeless.

The next morning Jacob, still wanting to appease Esau, sent even more gifts of animals and servants. By nightfall, he was left with only his family and two maidservants. Jacob was still not at peace! He sensed God's calling to set up camp for his family, and departed to be with the Lord (Genesis 32:22–23). During this journey, Jacob had spent much of his time and resources in trying to protect his family, and yet here we see him, in the middle of the night, leaving them unprotected in unfamiliar territory. Why? Because he was being called into a deeper relationship of trust with the Lord his God.

It was time for Jacob to show that he trusted God to fulfil His promise. I'm sure that Jacob's heart was in his mouth as he walked away from his family, in order to relate only to Jehovah Jirah, his provider. Jacob wrestled all night with our Lord God (Genesis 32:23). There are times in our lives when we are called to wrestle with God, but not wrestle *against* God; our natural being does that very easily without any special calling! To wrestle *with* God is to use all of our strength in order to meet with the one true living God – not only to know His promises, but also to know His heart and to know His character. And our hearts and characters are transformed in the process. Because of this time of wrestling with God, and the change in character that the encounter had produced, Jacob's name was to be changed from 'supplanter' to Israel, 'Prince with God' (Genesis 32:28). God waits patiently for each of us to learn to let go – and let God!

Our wrestling experience may not be in the same category as Jacob's wrestling for life, but it is, nonetheless, important. A common relationship that people wrestle with God about is boy/girlfriend issues. Friends of mine were happily going out together when Becky, the girlfriend, became ill with ME, a debilitating sickness. Returning to her parents' home to be nursed, her boyfriend, John, visited every weekend, regularly praying for Becky's healing until he was called to wrestle with God. John was directed to break off the relationship with Becky, and to force her out of her comfort-zone, giving her a need to receive God's healing. If John had chosen to wrestle against God's instructions, Becky could still be in her sick-bed now. Instead, she is John's perfectly healed wife and mother of their two children.

Having come to the place of a right relationship with God, Jacob was now ready to meet his brother. And when you see the reunion, you just know that it was the work of God:

> 'But Esau ran to meet him, and embraced him, and fell on his neck and kissed him, and they wept.' (Genesis 33:4)

Only God! The rugged man who avenged to kill Jacob was now kissing his neck! What a transformation! I believe that family reconciliation is so important to the Lord. A lesser disagreement can divide two friends and God allows them to never relate again. And yet, in families, the Lord seems to prepare a special time of reconciliation. Of course, we have the choice whether or not to respond! In the case of Jacob and Esau, not only were they able to dwell together peacefully, but also later, when Esau realised there wasn't enough room for both of their many possessions, he moved to the land of Canaan, acknowledging Jacob his rightful inheritance.

When Jacob settled in the land of Canaan, buying a plot of land in the city of Shechem, he erected an altar there and called it *'El Elohe Israel'* which translates 'God, the God of Israel' (Genesis 33:20). Whatever God gives to us, we need to immediately dedicate back to Him, thanking Him for His kind provision and merciful protection. Soon, however, Jacob's daughter, Dinah, was to be defiled by the son of a local prince, who then requested Jacob's permission for her to become his wife. Dinah's brothers, of course, were livid that their sister had been defiled in such a way, but still consented to the prince's request for his son to receive Dinah as wife. General intermarriage between the family of Israel and the Canaanites was permitted, but only if the men of the city were circumcised. Dinah's two full-brothers, however, revenged themselves, by slaying the men of the city while they were weak from the operation, plundering their goods and taking their wives and children, all without the permission of their father, Jacob.

Jacob's immediate response was one of fear, believing that the people of the nations would gather to destroy him and his family. The Lord told him to return to Bethel, the place where the Lord God had appeared to him when he'd fled from Esau. God will often call us back, or recall our attention, to the place where He acted to save us in a similar situation. Whereas Jacob ran away from Esau's juvenile threats, the Lord had Jacob travel through the land. The Canaanites and the Perizzites wanted revenge for the blood of their people (Genesis 34:30), yet the fear of God was upon them, and they were rendered incapable, for *'the terror of God was upon the cities that were all around them, and they did not pursue the sons of Jacob'* (Genesis 35:5). The family of Jacob would have perished, except that the Lord was on their side. This incident could be likened to situations in many a mature Christian's life. In the past, we've known the voice of God, His comfort and promises. God, we learnt, was our Deliverer. Yet, even in maturity, there are times when we react on instinct. We have to work at getting back to our 'Bethel', keeping our eyes focused on our First Love. The first time we met Jesus, we may have been running away from our fears. In the call to maturity, we are now called to walk through the midst of them. Scary, but possible!

So, Jacob made his way to Bethel and dwelt there. It wasn't to be a quick visit, but neither did Jacob settle there forever. We live our spiritual lives with the Lord in seasons; there is a season to stay and a season to go. There are times when we are called to push on and to work hard, and there are times when we are called aside, to rest awhile. If you constantly live in only one of these spheres, the chances are you are being directed by the flesh, rather than by the Spirit. We should not work so hard for the Lord that we never enjoy the presence of the Lord in the work, nor should we demand the Lord's comfort so much so, that we never get involved in doing His work.

God repeats with Jacob the name-changing ceremony; *'Your name is Jacob; your name shall not be called Jacob anymore, but Israel shall be your name'* (Genesis 35:10). The author tells us, *'So He* [the

LORD] *called his name Israel'* (Genesis 35:10). The Lord called Jacob Israel, but the author continues to call him Jacob. If the author continues to call the man Jacob, then we can presume that everyone else did so too. This scripture holds great significance. Jacob was known as a supplanter; one who displaces another. Jacob's sons killed the men of a whole city and took the women, children and livestock, but Jacob would have been held responsible. In his youth, the voice of his brother, Esau, called out against him, *'Is he not rightly named Jacob?'* (Genesis 27:36). Now, Jacob had to suffer the pressure of a whole nation thinking the same. God's words are full of comfort and encouragement to Jacob such as, 'that's your name, but to me you're a prince, and you always will be. I will call you Israel, Prince with God.' Whatever the terror of man's voice against you, be it thunderous accusations or vindictive whispering, pale into significance when God tells you how He feels about you. In our sorrow of being unjustly treated and misunderstood, our Daddy will shower blessings upon us, washing away our pain with comforting words of how precious, how delightful, and how beautiful we are to Him. That's why it is so important to follow the call back to our own personal Bethel, to experience anew the wonder of a deep encounter with our Almighty God and Father.

The Lord never revealed anything new to Jacob at Bethel, but confirmed what He had previously shared with him. God's promises are to become our dreams, but they can take a long time in materialising, and if we don't revisit them often enough, then we'll discard them as 'pipe dreams', instead of recognising them as the 'power dreams' that they are intended to be. For, with God all things are possible! God's promises, according to our natural mind, at best sound improbable, and at worst, impossible. The only way we can live to see the fulfilment of God's promises is to spend enough time with the Lord to allow Him to convince us that they are true.

The Lord did not reveal any new promises to Jacob, but He revealed Himself in a new and deeper way. The first time the Lord appeared to Jacob at Bethel, He did so in a dream. By the second visit to Bethel, the Lord was appearing and speaking with a conscious Jacob. As Jacob had matured, the Lord had been able to reveal more of Himself to him. He is gracious, training up His people gradually, and relates towards us with wisdom and compassion. A lady I once knew was very bitter about having become what she perceived as mature; she claimed that God had left her alone. But a call to maturity is not so much God's request for us to cope with the difficult circumstances alone, but rather, it is a call to willingness to lay down our difficulties in order to travel into His presence. The Lord always wants to be the centre of our world; He wants to be our burden-bearer; He promises never to leave us nor forsake us, and He desires to be our all in all. As Jacob found out, no problem is too big for God – not ever!

After his stay in Bethel, Israel travelled *'and pitched his tent beyond the tower of Eder'* (Genesis 35:21). Along the way, Rachel died in childbirth. Then Reuben, Jacob's first born, slept with Bilhah, Jacob's concubine, and mother of Reuben's half-brothers, Dan and Naphtali, and *'Israel heard about it'* (Genesis 35:22), yet showed no response. When another wrongs us, we travel through many different emotions. It may be that as Israel sought the Lord and shared his pain and sorrow, God placed it in his heart to do nothing about the incident. It is a struggle when in the natural you want justice, vengeance, or proof of repentance and change, and God in His wisdom says 'let go' and directs you to continue the relationship as if the offence never took place. Or perhaps Jacob, the supplanter, didn't know how to react to being wrongfully supplanted by his son. Being able to suggest two very different reasons for Jacob's silence brings home to me the truth that you cannot judge another man's actions from without, for from that angle you cannot possibly know and understand his reasons. That's why God judges the heart, not the action or reaction; the action is merely a by-product, and the attitude of the heart, the source.

Later, when Jacob's favourite son, Joseph (Rachel's firstborn), spoke of a dream in which his family bowed down before him, Jacob corrected Joseph, but then *'kept the matter in mind'* (Genesis 37:11). Like Mary, the mother of Jesus, when shepherds revealed truths about Jesus (Luke 2:19), Jacob was not to reject Joseph's words, but rather ponder them. How horrendous for Jacob to hear of his favourite son's apparent death. Often, when someone young dies suddenly, we cannot understand, and find ourselves asking, 'Why, God, Why?' This must have been especially so for Jacob, who kept Joseph's dreams in mind. He would not have been able to reconcile thoughts of prophetic dreams with the 'reality' of a premature, gruesome death. We are told Jacob mourned for his son, and would not be comforted by any of his other children. To grieve is healthy, a time to let out all the anguish, disappointment and pain, and to say goodbye. But many of us don't achieve this, by either blocking the grieving process (being unwilling or unable to feel or express emotion), or by becoming involved in the grieving process, only to get caught up in the emotion and unable to let go. Jacob was of the latter grouping, speaking over himself, *'I shall go down into the grave to my son in mourning'* (Genesis 37:35). In effect, Jacob was saying that he would no longer live his life day by day, but rather dedicate his life to mourning the loss of his son's life. Our God is the giver of life. When we cannot accept someone else's death, we are not able to fully accept our own life, and that has to have ill-effect on our relationship with the Lord, the Giver of life. When I was a child, my sister Marion and her children died in a house-fire. Ten years later, I began to walk with the Lord, but I did not live in the fullness of His blessings because I too, dedicated my life to mourning my loss. To become free has taken a lot of years, and a lot of counsel, freeing Marion to be with Jesus, and freeing myself to live my life as God intended.

Jacob probably blamed himself for sending Joseph to his brothers: if only he'd kept him home, then he'd be alive! Jacob thought that God was his family's protector, but that promise appeared to have been quashed. We can see these thoughts in Jacob's mind years later when his eldest ten sons travelled to Egypt for food, only to return minus one son and a request from 'the ruler' to see Jacob's youngest son, Benjamin. Of course, as we read the story, we have the benefit of knowing that 'the ruler' is Joseph, who desired to see his little brother, Benjamin. For Jacob, however, the request was too much. He declared,

> *'... My son shall not go down with you, for his brother is dead, and he is left alone. If any calamity should befall him along the way in which you go, then you would bring down my gray hair with sorrow to the grave.'* (Genesis 42:38)

Let us remember that Benjamin was not a child at this stage, but a man, for over twenty years had passed since his brothers sold Joseph into slavery.

Jacob had never been able to let go of Joseph and had, perhaps, unknowingly put pressure on Benjamin to take his brother's place. When we cannot allow ourselves to let go, we become controlling, and fear is our driving force. Even when the famine was severe in the land and the family's only hope of buying grain was to return to Egypt, Jacob refused to send Benjamin. Jacob, in this area of his life, no longer allowed God to be Lord. He was afraid to let go of Benjamin by allowing him to travel to Egypt. If Benjamin was out of Jacob's sight, then some misadventure could take place and he could die. Only at home, under Jacob's watchful eye could he be safe. Logically, this is untrue; misadventures happen at home too. But when you're governed by fear, logic is not one of your strong points!

Jacob struggled to trust his 'Son of the Right Hand' to God's protection, eventually agreeing to allow Benjamin to travel to Egypt, saying to his sons, *'may God Almighty give you mercy before the man, that he may release your other brother and Benjamin'* (Genesis 43:14). Jacob's words sounded promising, like a prayer of faith, but then his heart wilted, *'If I am bereaved, I am bereaved!'* (Genesis 43:14). Having let go of control, he also let go of hope. This emphasises that it is not the letting go that is helpful, but the letting go to God. There are many ways of letting go – from temporary release by 'drowning your sorrows' in alcohol, to a more permanent 'release' in choosing to block out the memories from the conscious mind. Yet, without giving the situation to God we cannot receive the gift of faith, which brings hope and comfort. Jacob had not yet reached that place.

In Egypt, Joseph was to reveal his identity to his brothers and send them home to inform Jacob that his son was still alive. We are told that, *'Jacob's heart stood still'* (Genesis 45:26). There have been similar cases throughout history when it has been believed that loved ones have been killed in battle, yet were still alive. Few, however, would have been kept waiting to hear the truth as long as Jacob. Joseph had spent thirteen years in prison and nine years as governor. Therefore, at least twenty-two years later, Jacob heard the amazing news. An old man could hardly take such a shock. It can therefore be expected that the heart would be affected. I'm no medical expert, but Jacob could have had a heart attack. As the sons assured him that this was all true, *'the spirit of Jacob their father revived'* (Genesis 45:27). God knew that Jacob's heart would stand still, but His plan was to strengthen him. Jacob, at one hundred and thirty years of age, arranged to travel to see his son, Joseph, before he died (Genesis 45:28).

On the way to Egypt, Jacob and his family stopped off at Beersheba to offer sacrifices to the God of his father Isaac (Genesis 46:1). This was a very special place for Jacob's family line. His grandfather, Abraham, had named the place Beersheba, meaning 'well of the oath', after making an oath of peace there with Abimelech whilst calling on the name of the Lord, the eternal God (Genesis 21:31-33). Jacob's father, Isaac, travelled there when the Philistines were continuously quarrelling with him, and the Lord appeared to him there to assure him of His presence and blessings (Genesis 26:24). Jacob, too, was to be assured of the Lord in this place.

The Lord began, *'I am God, the God of your father'* (Genesis 46:3). Jacob knew the story of God's revelation to his father, Isaac, at Beersheba. When God said, *'I'm the God of your father'*, he was saying, 'I'm the God who protected and provided for your father and I'll protect you.' If we met a man who was one-tenth as faithful towards our parents as the Lord God is, we'd take notice of him! This introduction was not for God's benefit, but for Jacob's – to fill him with faith and expectancy, and to rekindle in his heart a trust of God. The Lord went on to say, 'Do not be afraid.' God does not command such a thing except there be a reason. We can conclude, therefore, that Jacob was afraid.

Unlike his sons, Jacob had not yet received the comfort of seeing his favourite son alive. He was probably full of questions such as, why did God allow Joseph to be taken captive to Egypt? And if God wanted to provide for them in this famine, why couldn't He do it in Canaan, the Promised Land, instead of Egypt? Also, how could his posterity inherit the Promised Land if they were not even dwelling in it? The Lord answered, *'do not fear to go down to Egypt, for I will make of you a great nation there. I will go down with you to Egypt, and I will also surely bring you* [your posterity] *up again'* (Genesis 46:3-4). Perhaps Jacob was wearied by the prospect of the journey to Egypt. His only desire was to see his son alive, but what if he couldn't survive the journey? The Lord continued, *'Joseph will put his hand on your eyes'* (Genesis 46:4). The word of the Lord always proves true; not only did Jacob see his favourite son, but also he went on to live seventeen years in Egypt, and on Jacob's deathbed:

> 'Then Joseph fell on his father's face, and wept over him, and kissed him.' (Genesis 50:1)

That first meeting of father and son in Egypt was, as one can expect, an emotional encounter. Joseph *'presented himself to him* [his father], *and fell on his neck and wept on his neck a good while'* (Genesis 46:29). Jacob, on seeing his son alive and well, was now quite content to die (Genesis 46:30). He was, after all, one hundred and thirty years old and most of us would agree that he deserved to rest! But his time was not yet!

Joseph, as an eminent figure in Egypt, soon presented his father to Pharaoh (Genesis 47:7). The first thing that Jacob did was to bless Pharaoh. Jacob may have quivered from time to time, unsure of God's plans, but he was not only wise enough to recognise the Lord's provision in all that Pharaoh had to offer, but he was also courageous enough to speak blessing from the one true God to a reigning infidel. Pharaoh asked Jacob how old he was. Jacob responded, *'The days of the years of my pilgrimage are one hundred and thirty years'* (Genesis 47:9). His life had been a pilgrimage, both for his people of Israel to enter the Promised Land, and also his own personal pilgrimage into eternal life. He went on to say that the years had been few and evil. Recounting his life, one could agree that he had ample evidence for this statement; he struggled through childhood, was labelled as a 'taker' at birth, and was part of a dysfunctional family with each parent openly favouring one child over the other. As a young man, he had had to escape his brother's wrath, only to be manipulated and used by his uncle. Up until the death of Rachel, he had also had to contend with his two wives bickering. From their competing, many unwanted children were born. Wild animals, Jacob believed, had killed the first son he had ever loved. Perhaps worse news was that in reality his sons had sold Joseph as a slave, and kept Jacob in a dark den of deception for over twenty years. Added to this was the trouble that some of his sons caused him.

All in all, it would be reasonable to suggest that Jacob had experienced his fair share of evil, and sadly, it was all through family relationships. However, Jacob could have equally proclaimed God's blessing in his life to Pharaoh, for the Lord had always protected and directed Jacob in his hour of need. However, reality or pessimism is not the issue here. We need to look deeper. This was a man in pain, not yet come to terms with the events in his life. The wounds were quite fresh and he still had a lot to work through. People from outside of the situation could be quick to criticise, thinking that Jacob should have been more grateful to God, and should have taken the opportunity to magnify God in his testimony before Pharaoh. The problem with this argument is that it comes from the head, and Jacob was speaking from the heart. They are on two different levels, and Jacob appearing to say the 'right thing' would not bring truth when only healing could do that. When the head alone speaks the 'truth', it is from a notion of religion. When the heart agrees with that same truth, it's founded in a knowledge of, and relationship with, the Lord. Then the spoken words have meaning and power.

To view Jacob's progression, let us look to his words seventeen years later on his death-bed, where he described his life to Joseph saying,

> '... *The God who has fed me all my life long to this day,*
> *The Angel who has redeemed me from all evil* ...'
> (Genesis 48:15–16)

Time had brought healing and understanding for Jacob. He did not deny the evil that had pursued his life, but he was able to put the greater emphasis on God's redemptive power. This statement was again from the heart. If we attempt to force people into grateful speeches, or pseudo-worship, then they may never know real gratitude and therefore, miss out on a real relationship with the Lord in their hearts. The Word says that He gives us *'the garment of praise for the spirit of heaviness'* (Isaiah 61:3). Of course, we must play our part in choosing to wear it, but far too often (it seems to me), people are forced to make the garment too! The Lord our God is a patient God who will stand by our sides continually, until we know His healing redemption in fullness and power. In the fullness of time, He will teach us all we need to know and understand.

Personal application

Jacob, on his first personal encounter with God, was transformed from a self-dependent youth to a man who trusted life events to God. However, we see a dramatic change in his character when Joseph was presumed dead. Jacob grieved the loss of his favourite son for over twenty years, surviving life rather than living it, and even when reunited with Joseph, he still needed to work through his grief. Finding Joseph alive brought healing to Jacob, but how can we, who will not find our loved ones miraculously alive, come into the fullness of life? This is a big issue, needing more than this short section to give it its full value, yet a few pointers might be helpful:

▶ There is what is known as a 'cycle of grief' – shock, numbness, anger, fear, relief, and acceptance are all emotions you may experience. There is no order to the cycle as we are all individuals experiencing our own particular loss. The relief of knowing about the cycle is that you begin to see that your reactions are 'normal'; there is nothing wrong with you just because you experience extremes of emotions.

- ▶ It's important to allow yourself to grieve. It may feel like it's going to last forever, but most people come to a place of acceptance after a year or so. Bottling up the emotions creates problems in other areas – e.g. physical illness or stormy relationships, so find a way of release. Find the best method of release for you. Some people like to talk regularly with a friend/counsellor. Others find keeping a journal of their thoughts and feelings helpful.

- ▶ Dealing with the spiritual issues of the death of someone close in no way negates the need to grieve, but frees us to grieve successfully. When my brother-in-law died last year, my sister and I prayed into the situation:
  - As Dennis died at home, a spirit of death remained there. We cast it out in Jesus' name.
  - Norah, naturally, was upset with her husband for leaving her, and with Jesus for taking him. She chose to forgive them both. She agreed to allow Jesus to take him, and said goodbye to Dennis.
  - We broke the soul-ties between husband and wife, and prayed that God, at this sad time, would bring joyful memories of their relationship. We began to share lovely memories we had of Dennis' gentle, kind nature, and thanked God for bringing him into our lives.
  - Norah was afraid of being alone. We prayed that the peace of God would fill her home, and asked Jesus to be her 'husband', her protector, her confidant, and her provider.

- ▶ The central focus of Christianity is that Jesus conquered death when He rose from the dead. He is the resurrection and the life through whom we have eternal life. Our emotions may question the validity of this claim as we suffer the pain of loss, but as we come back into relationship with the Lord, we are comforted by His assurances that in heaven, we will be together again with those we love.

Chapter 13
Lost and Found: Jacob and Esau

We are first introduced to Jacob and Esau when they are in the womb. Even in that safe haven they struggled against each other. Rebekah, their mother, received a 'verbal scan' from the Lord – that they struggled against each other because they were two nations, and that the younger would be greater than the elder; indeed the elder would serve the younger. Even on the journey down the birth canal, Jacob had grabbed hold of his older brother, Esau's heel. His parents, therefore, presented him with the name that translated means 'supplanter', or one who supersedes another. Jacob was just born, and yet it was already obvious that he was to take the place of the firstborn. So did that mean that everyone would treat him with the respect of the firstborn? No – this is not a story of plain sailing. For it seems that wherever there is relationship, there will also be conflict!

As the boys grew and their personalities developed, the parents each chose their favourite son. Esau, a 'man's man', who was a skilful hunter and strong and hairy, was his father's favourite. Jacob, a mild man who preferred to dwell in tents, was gentle-natured and soft skinned. He was his mother, Rebekah's, favourite child. It is not long before we have the opportunity to view the twins' lack of closeness. Jacob had cooked a stew and Esau, arriving from the field hungry, asked Jacob for some of his food. There was no love lost between the two brothers as Jacob responded, *'Sell me your birthright'* (Genesis 25:31). What a high price to pay for a bowl of stew! Esau could have refused this ridiculous offer, yet he succumbed to fleshly desire and paid the asking price. Esau ate, drank, and left, despising his birthright (Genesis 25:34). His excuse for agreeing to the exchange was that he was about to die, thus his birthright would be of little value to him. He may have felt like the frustrated Prince of England,

Charles, who, according to the media, wonders if his ageing mother will ever depart in time for him to benefit from his birthright! Alternatively, Esau could simply have felt so famished that he allowed himself the indulgence of exaggeration. Whatever his reasoning, Esau abhorred his birthright. What went wrong? Did he not receive adequate teaching of his spiritual inheritance, or had he attaching little value to the teaching that he had received? Whatever the cause of this major mistake in Esau's life, he was to find out that he had a hefty price to pay.

In handing over his birthright to Jacob, Esau had cursed his own inheritance. When the time came for Isaac to bless his firstborn he called for Esau, and sent him out to hunt venison in order to make a feast for his father. The scene had to be set for such an auspicious occasion! However, Rebekah, on overhearing Isaac, began to plot a cunning plan to present Jacob as Esau, so that he could receive the blessing instead. While Esau was hunting deer, Rebekah told Jacob to follow her commands. Speed was needed – Jacob was to bring two kid goats, and Rebekah would transform them into 'venison'. In England, during World War Two, mothers were given recipe ideas on how to disguise cheap, accessible food as more luxurious, unavailable foods; Rebekah was presumably following the same procedure. By using the correct cooking method, spices and appropriate marinade, Jacob would soon be able to present 'venison' to his father.

Jacob, being nothing like his brother, was obviously fearful that his father would find him out, and that he would end up with a curse rather than a blessing. Rebekah, nevertheless, was determined that this plan should go ahead, and resolved to shoulder any curse received. Jacob was to wear Esau's best outfit and be covered in goatskin. When dressed to deceive his father, Jacob did not attempt to disguise his own voice, and so Isaac recognised the voice to be that of Jacob. As Isaac was becoming blind he therefore asked to touch 'Esau'. The boy felt and smelt like Esau so, after eating, Isaac blessed Jacob with the blessing of the firstborn. This was a beautiful blessing, comprising the provision of Almighty God in food and drink, respect from peoples and nations, a divine protection in that whoever blessed or cursed Jacob would receive likewise, but also that his brother would serve him (Genesis 27:27–29).

As soon as Jacob left, Esau arrived to receive the blessing. As Isaac realised that he had been deceived into giving Jacob the firstborn's blessing, there was a joining together of despair between father and son; Isaac trembled and Esau cried bitterly. Esau criticised Jacob saying, *'Is he not rightly named Jacob? For he has supplanted me these two times. He took away my birthright, and now look, he has taken away my blessing!'* (Genesis 27:36). Esau, however, had conveniently forgotten the part that he'd played in losing his birthright. Jacob did not use cunning devices to take Esau's birthright, but had openly offered an exchange. Esau, of his own freewill, chose to sell his birthright to Jacob. The blessing he was now devastated to have lost was actually part of the birthright with which he'd paid for a bowl of stew, just as if you sell a house, you cannot then expect to live in it. Esau showed a lack of maturity in blaming everything on Jacob, and even avenged to kill him. However, Jacob was not without fault either. Even though God had told Rebekah that Jacob would be greater than Esau, and that Esau would serve Jacob, it can never be said that God chooses deception to bring about His divine plan; deception is the work of Satan with the cooperation of man. Too often, we can justify ungodly reactions to situations by claiming God's providence. In fact, we are cutting right across the Lord's provision as we strive to provide for ourselves. If we can only learn to wait for God to fulfil His promises! No matter how entrepreneurial we become in attempting to gain God's promises, we will not succeed until we lay it all down and acknowledge our Lord God as the only source of our provision. And Jacob, no less than the rest of us, had to live according to this spiritual law.

Isaac believed he was about to die, and Esau was ready to kill Jacob. Rebekah, wanting to protect her son, persuaded Isaac to send Jacob to her family to find a bride. Over the next twenty years, we follow Jacob's life, while we hear nothing of Esau. When it was time for Jacob to return to the land of his father, on nearing his homeland, he sent the rest of the family ahead while he remained behind to be alone with God (Genesis 32). Jacob had already sent messengers to his brother, Esau, along with gifts to find favour with him. He had met with angels (Genesis 32:1), but the news that Esau was coming to meet him with four hundred men left him *'greatly afraid and distressed'* (Genesis 32:7); quickly dividing the party in two, he hoped that one group would at least survive. He also prayed, reminding God of His promises and asking His deliverance. Reminding God of all His promises during our times of uncertainty is beneficial, not for God, but for us, for *'faith comes by hearing, and hearing by the word of God'* (Romans 10:17). Hearing the proclamation, therefore, we receive an assurance that God (who not being human is therefore incapable of lying) will fulfil His promises and will deliver us. Furthermore, attacking spirits hear our confession of God's promises; there is power in the Word, and as we speak it, they are forced to retreat.

When we seek God's deliverance, be it spiritual or physical, He will often direct us to the best action. Sending his family on ahead so he could be alone with the Lord, Jacob learnt to wait on God. He wrestled with God with all his might saying, *'I will not let You go unless You bless me'* (Genesis 32:26). Without the blessing of God, Jacob knew that Esau was well able to destroy him, to chew him up and spit him out! No manmade plan could save Jacob. It was only the intervention of God! It may well have been Esau's intention to destroy Jacob and his posterity as he set out with four hundred men, but a transformation had already taken place by the time he reached Jacob. No longer the distraught youth vowing vengeance, he ran to meet Jacob, embraced him, fell on his neck, and kissed him. Together, Jacob and Esau wept (Genesis 33:4). Only God can perform such a miracle of reconciliation! These two were never close, not even in the womb, yet here they were weeping together. Look, what God can do when we hand the situation over to Him!

It saddens me greatly to hear of brothers and sisters in Christ who, by the grace of God, have been closer than natural siblings, yet have lost their relationship through disputes. However, it has happened throughout Christian history. Paul and Barnabas, having worked together over many years, allowed argument to become *'so sharp that they parted from one another'* (Acts 15:39). Their contention was over whether a young man called Mark, who had previously left a mission before it was complete, should accompany them on another journey. Barnabas was determined to take Mark, and Paul insisted they shouldn't. They both thought that they were right and the other wrong, but it was contention and not the will of God, that separated them. We never hear of them reuniting, but in Paul's letter to Timothy he asked that Mark should be sent to him claiming *'he is useful to me for ministry'* (2 Timothy 4:11); as Mark matured, perhaps Paul recognised his error. In the story of Jacob and Esau, we have natural brothers (who never expressed love towards one another), being united by the love of God. May the Lord choose to reconcile brothers and sisters in Christ who, although they may have deeply loved one another, have allowed contention to separate them.

From then on, Jacob and Esau dwelt in the same land, both receiving the blessings of increase of wealth until their assets were too great to be contained. What happened? Did Esau claim the right over *his* homeland? The amazing answer is 'No'. Esau, realising the problem, chose to move to another country, he and all he had. Esau took a side step, freeing Jacob to receive the blessings that were promised by Almighty God. In so doing, Esau put himself in the right place to receive his blessing from God – to become a separate nation he needed to be in a separate place. Jacob's time alone with God brought about this miracle. When we can lay down all that has happened before, and cry out to God for His mercy upon messed-up relationships, this episode shows that God can, and does, turn things around;

> '... all things work together for good to those who love God, to those who are called according to His purpose.' (Romans 8:28)

Amen!

Personal application

Brothers that had a tempestuous relationship as youths were blessed with a heart-warming reunion in later life. The power of reconciliation came from Jacob calling out to God for their relationship. Jacob's only request was that the Lord would deliver him from his brother's wrath. However, he was praying to the God *'who is able to do exceedingly abundantly above all that we ask or think, according to the power that works in us'* (Ephesians 3:20).

Contention in the body of Christ, sibling against sibling, is the work of Satan. Although the Lord blesses our willingness to work for Him after a break-up with brothers/sisters in Christ, He never blesses a spirit of condemnation or judgment. Paul, in writing to the Corinthians after hearing a bad report regarding their behaviour, does not say 'I disown you' but *'I determined not to know anything among you except Jesus Christ and Him crucified'* (1 Corinthians 2:2). The message of salvation through the cross of Jesus needs to penetrate every area of our lives, and every relationship. We need to put the cross of Jesus between friends/

enemies and ourselves. The cross of Jesus says that we need to forgive when we want to judge, and to release a person/ministry into God's blessings when we want to hold them in condemnation. If we die to our self as we are commanded, then we will not be so proud as to condemn another person.

Jacob and Esau were able to dwell together in the same land after their reconciliation. Those desiring reconciliation with a brother or sister, but who can only sense antagonism from the other party, can be encouraged by Jacob's prayer. God answered *one* person's prayer to reconcile *two* people. God's heart is for unity in the Church so, as you come in line with His heart's desire, your prayer will certainly be answered in the fullness of time.

Chapter 14

Love Triangle: Jacob, Rachel and Leah

Jacob, on being sent to live with his Uncle Laban, found himself at a well in the right vicinity. As he enquired of his uncle, he was told that Laban's daughter, Rachel, was approaching with Laban's sheep. Jacob's immediate response was to order the shepherds to remove the stone from the well in order to give the sheep water. Perhaps he wanted them to be busy so that he could relate more freely with Rachel. Or maybe he was eager to help Rachel water the flock. Jacob had obviously been brought up to give servants orders, but these shepherds refused with universal assertion – 'that's not the way we do it around here!'

Jacob took it upon himself to remove the stone from the well and water Laban's flock. Only after this, did Jacob kiss Rachel and tell her who he was. This had given Rachel time to view this stranger. What must she have thought? Was he perceived as a kind man, or a possible suitor? For Jacob, the incident was enough to make him weep. Doubtless, he would have heard the story of the day that his mother had come to a well to collect water, and thus met Abraham's servant through whom she was betrothed to marry Jacob's father, Isaac. Now, Jacob had arrived at the gateway of his own love story; before him stood his cousin, a beautiful woman, whom Jacob loved and offered seven years of work for.

A beautiful illustration of Jacob's love for Rachel was that the seven years *'seemed only a few days to him'* (Genesis 29:20). Love, it seems, bore the fruit of patience for Jacob, with the frustration of waiting having no hold over him. Within each of us, then, is the potential for patience for *'love suffers long and is kind'*

(1 Corinthians 13:4). God, who is Love, dwells within each born-again, Spirit-filled Christian. When we are led by Love, as we wait for His promises to be fulfilled, the years pass by as if only a few days. I am in the third year of a period of waiting, a time in which my number one priority is taking care of my Mum. Socialising opportunities are sporadic, church involvement even less often, but while I look forward to returning to an active church life, I could not be happier than I am now – ministering to my Mum until, as God says, 'the work is complete'. However, when we strive for our dreams to become reality we are not quite in step with our Lord's plans. The solution is in our hands; we need to give God's plans back to Him, the great Organiser, worshipping and adoring Him, and choosing to trust our Lord to fulfil His great plans for us (Jeremiah 29:11).

Having waited patiently for seven years to receive Rachel as his wife, Jacob was given Leah instead, conveniently hidden behind a veil. As soon as Jacob realised Laban's deceitful act, he contended the agreement with Laban, who argued that it was not customary to marry the younger before the firstborn. Rachel, as much as Jacob, would have looked forward to the 'big day', yet Leah probably dreaded it, fearing being the 'frumpy big sister left on the shelf!' She, doubtless, was relieved to take the place of Rachel, possibly expecting to be Jacob's only wife. However, to appease Jacob, Laban offered to give Rachel too, after only seven days, for the price of another seven years' labour. Rachel must have been devastated on the wedding night when she was kept away from Jacob, but as she was soon to discover, she would always be number one wife to him for *'he also loved Rachel more than Leah'* (Genesis 29:30). Her younger sister, in all probability, superseded any authority which Leah had hoped to claim as the first wife. Being in Rachel's shadow was an affliction for Leah. Bearing Jacob's first son she proclaimed, *'The LORD has surely looked on my affliction. Now therefore, my husband will love me'* (Genesis 29:32). We can glean from the names that she gave to subsequent sons that she never received the love from Jacob that she longed for. Even on the birth of her sixth son, Leah hoped to gain a greater claim to her husband's attention; *'Now my husband will dwell with me'* (Genesis 30:20). Poor Leah, though always striving, could never attain her goal. As God never intended children to be used as tools of bribery, her scheming could never be blessed.

While these numerous births made little impact upon Jacob, it affected Rachel enormously. Unable to conceive, and from a heart of envy, she cried out to her husband, *'Give me children, or else I die'* (Genesis 30:1). Jacob's anger was aroused against her saying, *'Am I in the place of God, who has withheld from you the fruit of the womb?'* (Genesis 30:2). Rachel, like Leah, was unable to find peace within her situation. In a society where barrenness would be seen as a curse, and the sufferer considered as less of a woman, she was unable to appreciate Jacob's love for her; while Jacob was obliged to take care of Leah and her children, he loved to take care of Rachel, with or without children. We also see in Rachel's response that she did not have a close relationship with the Lord. Instead of praying for a child, Rachel gave her maid to Jacob to bear children on her behalf. Even before the plan was put into action, Rachel was anticipating a number of sons to be born upon her knee – sons that she could claim as her own.

Caught up in their rivalry, both Rachel and Leah were consumed by jealousy and competitiveness. Instead of being a blessing from God, children were treated as commodities in the sister's private battle. Eventually, however, God's goodness and mercy prevailed:

> *'Then God remembered Rachel, and God listened to her and opened her womb.'* (Genesis 30:22)

We are not told if Rachel made a request to the Lord directly, or if He heard her heart cry. But, just look at the backdrop of jealousy and bitterness, and see what a faithful, loving God we serve. One who does not count our sins before us, but mercifully gives us our heart's desire. He is so wonderful!

At last Joseph was born, Jacob's eleventh son. Rachel believed, and therefore claimed, *'The Lord shall add to me another son'* (Genesis 30:24). Indeed, God granted to Rachel a second son, Benjamin, but unfortunately Rachel was not to be blessed in watching her son grow up. This is because her beloved Jacob had inadvertently cursed her. Jacob, seeing that he was no longer in favour with Laban, called Rachel and Leah to discuss his plan to return to his homeland without informing their father. While packing, Rachel stole her father's idols. When Laban eventually caught up with Jacob, he accused Jacob of taking his house-gods. Having no knowledge of these foreign objects of idolatry being in the camp, let alone in Rachel's tent, Jacob announced, *'with whomever you find your gods, do not let him live'* (Genesis 31:32).

Evil may often take life, but Satan must first get permission from God to kill and to destroy (Job 2:6). Rachel had hidden the idol in her camel's saddle, and then sat upon it:

> 'And she said to her father, "Let it not displease my lord that I cannot rise before you, for the manner of woman is with me."'
> (Genesis 31:35)

Jacob's words were filled with power and authority and so Rachel would therefore die for stealing the idols. Having come out of the protection of her husband's covering, her guilt brought her under the spiritual authority of his curse. Rachel used the 'time of woman' as an excuse not to stand when hiding the idol from her father, and so in a greater time of woman – labour – she died. In using womanhood as a tool of deception to hide the false god, she was handing over the rights concerning her womanhood to Satan, the power behind every false god. How sad for Jacob and Rachel that their romance, tinged throughout with family problems, had to come to this premature end.

Rachel, aware that she was dying in labour, named her child, 'Ben-Oni' meaning 'Son of my Sorrow'. Yet Jacob, caring for the son of the mother as much as he cared for the mother herself, renamed his son Benjamin, meaning 'Son of the Right Hand'. This was done to protect his son from the ungodly burden of guilt that surrounded his mother's death. For God alone can give and take life. If this was the end of Rachel's life, what became of her sister, Leah? Sadly, Leah is never mentioned again. Her whole reason for being mentioned was rivalry with her sister. Even her death is not mentioned, indicating how unimportant she had become. She was, however, to share a grave with Jacob; a small victory as the spirit and soul were no longer present in the lifeless bodies.

Personal application

Within this story are two important elements of life – marital and sibling relationships. Very few of us have to simultaneously contend with the issues that each relationship entails as Jacob and his wives did. Yet, the issue of sibling rivalry is a very real threat to our Christian walk; allowing it to control our lives, we are controlled by our own sinful nature. We are more blessed than Rachel or Leah, for we have the Holy Spirit to teach, guide, and correct us. It is very difficult for any of us to correct a stale relationship, but God who is Love is able:

> *'Love suffers long and is kind; love does not envy; love does not parade itself, is not puffed up; does not behave rudely, does not seek its own, is not provoked, thinks no evil; does not rejoice in iniquity, but rejoices in the truth; bears all things, believes all things, hopes all things, endures all things. Love never fails ... '*
> (1 Corinthians 13:4–8)

Consider a relationship that, time and again, you fail within. Perhaps patience is lacking, or you are easily provoked. By the power of God's love, the relationship can be turned around:

- Trust to God the difficult relationship that you would like to see improved.

- Soul-ties are formed in every relationship. They are spiritual tubing that connect you, and through which you receive and deliver each other's soul beliefs. Ungodly soul-ties are formed through relating incorrectly, whilst right relationships form godly soul-ties.
  Pray this:

  > *In Jesus name, I break the ungodly soul-tie between* [name the person] *and me, drawing back to me all that belongs to me, and sending back to* [person's name] *all that belongs to him/her. I pray for the godly soul-tie, all that is good in our relationship, to be strengthened. Amen.*

- Allow God to show you the root of your problem; e.g. anger over parental preference. You need to release the past to be released from its hold over you – therefore, allow Jesus to bring your pain to the surface, and release it to the Lord, choosing to forgive the person who hurt you. The Holy Spirit may also bring to your remembrance your own sin and need for forgiveness. It is important not only to ask God's forgiveness, but also to forgive yourself.

- Commit the continuous relationship to God, asking for God's grace to lead you in a practical way out of the battlefield, e.g. to not be provoked into an angry response. In a stale relationship, many responses will be habitual. Allow Jesus to be Lord of your responses – give Him the ownership papers that allow Him to break ungodly habits.

- Ask the Lord if a special time of reconciliation would be appropriate to openly forgive one another and wipe the slate clean to begin again. Sometimes, as in the case of abuse, this may not be God's plan for you, and He would rather strengthen your relationship with people who respect and care for you.

Chapter 15
Meet the Tribes: Jacob and Sons

On his deathbed, Israel spoke to each son (and the tribe that they would father) a blessing or a curse, *'each one according to his own blessing'* (Genesis 49:28), in respect of life choices that they had made. Therefore, by studying Jacob's dying words, we may discern God's 'tongue', by Jacob proclaiming the future of each of the tribes of Israel. But also, we receive revelation about the relationships that he shared with each of his sons.

The firstborn, recognised as a father's might and the beginning of his strength, and the excellency of dignity and of power (Genesis 49:3), becomes successor to his father as the head of the family or tribe, and is given a double portion of all that his father has (Deuteronomy 21:17). Reuben, Jacob's firstborn son, dishonoured his father by sleeping with Bilhah, Jacob's concubine, and so lost the privileges of the firstborn; *'because he defiled his father's bed, his birthright was given to the sons of Joseph'* (1 Chronicles 5:1). We can hear Jacob's pain, even forty years after the event, as he announces to Reuben's brothers, *'He went up to my couch'* (Genesis 49:4).

Reuben was degraded by his father, but not disowned or disinherited. He lost his birthright, but was still to receive the privileges of a son. Instead of the blessing of the firstborn to excel above his brothers, Jacob prophesied that the tribe of Reuben would never excel because Reuben's sin showed him to be as *'unstable as water'* (Genesis 49:4). Without the desire to excel, the tribe of Reuben, during the Exodus, chose to receive their inheritance on 'the other side' of the Jordan, rather than to continue on to the Promised Land (Joshua 14:3). There is no recording of any of the tribe of Reuben becoming judge, prophet or priest, and the only descendants of any renown (Dathan, Abiram and On), were made famous for their profane rebellion against Moses

(Numbers 16). Here is a strong example of how a parent's behaviour will affect the lives of their children; the descendants of Reuben were to be cursed because of his grave sin. Also, we are able to reflect on the quality that enables a person to excel. So often, we consider it impossible to excel without outstanding talent, yet Reuben's reason for never succeeding was because he was unstable. To excel, therefore, we do not need great talents, but stability. As a teacher and nanny, I have known amazingly talented children who failed to channel their gifts successfully because they have lacked discipline, and others who, through commitment rather than talent, have achieved great success.

Two other sons who incurred a grave sin against their father were Simeon and Levi. When Jacob first returned to Canaan, Shechem, the son of the prince of the country, dishonoured Jacob's daughter, Dinah. After some discourse, Jacob and his sons agreed to allow Shechem to marry Dinah if he and the men of the city were circumcised. However, while the men were recovering from the pain of the operation, Dinah's full-brothers, Simeon and Levi, being angry and revengeful, broke into the city to kill all the men, taking women and children, possessions and livestock. Jacob was furious with his two sons for creating problems with the inhabitants of Canaan, but Simeon and Levi felt justified responding, *'Should he treat our sister like a harlot?'* (Genesis 34:31).

The Lord taught Jacob to trust Him through this experience, as the whole family travelled safely to Bethel (House of God), past neighbouring cities full of potential enemies, but Jacob could never trust these two sons ever again. On his deathbed, possibly half a century later, wounds that Simeon and Levi's behaviour had caused him were still evident (Genesis 49:5–7). Because of their barbarous killing of the Shechemites, Jacob declared that *'Instruments of cruelty are in their dwelling place'* (Genesis 49:5). Swords were seen as tools of protection, but Simeon and Levi had chosen to slaughter a city that could not defend itself. Making clear that he had nothing to do with orchestrating Simeon and Levi's vengeful act, Jacob separated himself from them:

> *'Let not my soul enter their counsel;*
> *Let not my honour be united to their assembly.'* (Genesis 49:6)

As a warning to future generations, similar advice can be found in the book of Proverbs:

> *'My son, do not walk in the way with them,*
> *Keep your foot from their path;*
> *For their feet run to evil,*
> *And they make haste to shed blood.'* (Proverbs 1:15–16)

Because of their sin, the tribes of Simeon and Levi were to be scattered amongst the other tribes (Genesis 49:7). Again, this prophecy is substantiated in the Scriptures. Simeon's inheritance was within the inheritance of the children of Judah (Joshua 19:1), and the Levites, as priests, were scattered amongst all the other tribes (Joshua 21:5–7). In Simeon's case, the sentence remained a curse because of their own irreverent actions, joining themselves to Baal of Peor through harlotry (Numbers 25:14). The sentence for the Levites, however, was to become a blessing. When the Israelites began to worship a golden calf, the Levites proved themselves to be *'on the LORD's side'* (Exodus 32:26), expressing zeal for the Lord our God and His statutes. Curses, therefore, can be reversed, for the Lord promises:

> *'And all these blessings shall come upon you, and overtake you, because you obey the voice of the LORD your God.'*
> (Deuteronomy 28:2)

To be scattered amongst the people of Israel, in worship of the great God, was therefore an honour and privilege for the descendants of Levi.

Judah received wonderful blessings from his father. His name means 'Praise', and Jacob affirmed, *'you are he whom your brothers shall praise'* (Genesis 49:8). Although Joseph's sons received the inheritance of the firstborn son, Judah was given the authority of the firstborn:

> *'Your hand shall be on the neck of your enemies;*
> *Your father's children shall bow down before you.'*
> (Genesis 49:8b)

Looking back to when Jacob's sons tried to persuade him to allow Benjamin to travel to Egypt, we realise that while Jacob would not heed the request of his firstborn son, Reuben, he eventually agreed to put his youngest son in the care of Judah (Genesis 42:37–38; 43:9–11). Already, perhaps, Judah possessed the authority and respect of the firstborn. Scripture again verifies

Jacob's blessing; Judah, the largest tribe, was chosen by God to lead the nation in conquering the Canaanites (Judges 1:2). The excellency of dignity and power, reserved for the firstborn, were in Judah's possession. Yet, unlike his three brothers before him, Judah's sin (Genesis 38) was not mentioned. On closer inspection, we may see that Judah, unlike his older brothers, repented of his sin. Repentance, therefore, has a spiritual power to catapult us out of the realm of curses into God's abundant blessings. A friend of mine who was once an antagonist of God's Word, through repentance, was blessed to become the Lord's mouthpiece.

The excellency which Jacob bestowed upon Judah inferred that one greater than Judah would come from his tribe. In time, *'Judah prevailed over his brothers, and from him came a ruler'* (1 Chronicles 5:2). Jesus Christ is the 'Lion of Judah' (Revelation 5:5) who conquers His Father's enemies and protects His father's children; He is the praise of the saints and the power and authority of the Father. Speaking prophetically of the Messiah's coming, Jacob declared,

> *'The scepter shall not depart from Judah,*
> *Nor a lawgiver from between his feet,*
> *Until Shiloh comes;*
> *And to Him shall be the obedience of the people.'*
>   (Genesis 49:10)

From the time of David's reign until the captivity, the sceptre remained in Judah and even after this, until Christ's coming, Judah possessed substantial authority. After the crucifixion of Christ Jesus, their authority was curtailed, and in the same century (AD 71), the temple was destroyed, just as Jesus had prophesied (Luke 19:43–44). The people of Israel were therefore scattered throughout the world. In Jesus' prophecy about Jerusalem's destruction, He wept over the ignorance of the people of that city:

> *'saying, "If you had known, even you, especially in this your day, the things that make for your peace! But now they are hidden from your eyes.'*   (Luke 19:42)

Jesus is our peace, and only through Christ can we truly know peace. Until the people of Israel realise that the Messiah has already come, they cannot enter His peace. Yet, even Caiaphas, the high priest *'prophesied that Jesus would die for the nation, and not for that nation only, but also that He would gather together in one the children of God who were scattered abroad'* (John 11:51–52). No matter how much God's chosen people refuse to acknowledge Jesus Christ as the Messiah, we are assured that Jesus, with the sceptre in His right hand, is the Lawgiver, and to Him shall be the gathering of the children of God, as He is lifted up from the earth (John 12:32).

Concerning Zebulun, Jacob prophesied the region and work of his posterity; they were to become sailors living by the border of Sidon (Genesis 49:13). This was confirmed in Moses' blessing of the tribe of Zebulun (Deuteronomy 33:19), and the division of land by lot (Joshua 19:11). To divide by lot is to allow 'chance' to make the decision. However, when one casts lots before the Lord as Joshua did, God designs the outcome. Here again, therefore, we have confirmation of Jacob's prophecy being the word of the Lord.

Jacob described Issachar as *'a strong donkey, lying down between two burdens'* (Genesis 49:14), evoking a picture of ease and contentment. Jacob continues, *'He saw that rest was good, and the land was pleasant'* (Genesis 49:15). Issachar, consequently, fathered a people who preferred to use their strength to toil the land rather than to go to war. The land allotted to them was, and still is, the richest in the area (Joshua 19:17–23); Esdraelon, a plain of rich soil, Mount Tabor, and Gilgoa, were within Issachar's borders, with the river Kishon running through it. As Jacob spoke of Issachar's future in the past tense, he prophesied,

> *'He bowed his shoulder to bear a burden,*
> *And became a band of slaves.'* (Genesis 49:15b)

Shalmaneser, king of Assyria from BC 730, carried the people of the land, including the tribe of Issachar, to Assyria to become slaves (2 Kings 17:6). Jacob predicted both Issachar's beginning and end, for after the captivity, Issachar was no longer known as a tribe.

Jacob spoke to Dan next, a son of Rachel's servant:

> *'Dan shall judge his people*
> *As one of the tribes of Israel.'* (Genesis 49:16)

We can conclude that being the son of a servant did not make

Dan inferior to Jacob's more 'legitimate' sons. He too, would become a judge of Israel. Yet, Dan was also to become

> 'A viper by the path,
> That bites the horse's heels
> So that its rider shall fall backward.' (Genesis 49:17)

When the Israelites entered the Promised Land, the Lord instructed them to destroy all of the inhabitants so that they could not pollute their worship of the one true, living God. Instead, by allowing the inhabitants to remain as slaves, the children of Israel were encouraged to worship foreign gods. Dan's disobedience to the Word of God was even greater, as on pursuing the Promised Land, the Danites stole manmade gods and began to worship them (Jude 18). Their open idolatry instigated spiritual division in Israel. Their idolatrous behaviour was encouraged by Jeroboam, king of Israel, who made an altar in the city of Dan and placed a golden calf upon it to deter the people of Israel from returning to Jerusalem in Judah to worship the one true, living God (1 Kings 12:25–33). Obviously, *'this thing became a sin'* (1 Kings 12:30).

Amos, the prophet, declared the judgment of God on the people who, by their adulterous acts, chose to rebel against God,

> *'Those who swear by the sin of Samaria,*
> *Who say,*
> *"As your god lives, O Dan" ...*
> *They shall fall and never rise again.'* (Amos 8:14)

The tribe of Dan, in introducing idolatry to the nation at the beginning of their conquest of Canaan could, for this reason, be seen as a snake that bites the heel of the horse, so that its rider (Israel) should fall backwards. The nation of Israel was later dispersed because of idolatry:

> *'And the LORD rejected all the descendants of Israel, afflicted them, and delivered them into the hand of plunderers, until He had cast them from His sight.'* (2 Kings 17:20)

In Revelation 7, the tribe of Dan is not mentioned with the 144,000 of the twelve tribes of Israel upon whom the seal of God approves. Dan's role in the destruction of the nation of Israel, God's chosen people, may be the reason for this.

Of Gad, Jacob declared:

> 'Gad, a troop shall trample upon him,
> But he shall triumph at last.' (Genesis 49:19)

Herein is a prophecy of encouragement for the tribe of Gad. After the exodus, Gad chose to remain on the east side of Jordan, in the country of Gilead, surrounded by the Moabites and the Ammonites (Deuteronomy 3:11–12). In many of the battles, the Moabites and the Ammonites were 'a troop that trampled upon them'. In the time of Saul and David, however, the Gadites joined forces with other Israelites to triumph over their enemies. Jacob's prophecy was realised when the Gadites *'cried out to God in the battle. He heeded their prayer, because they put their trust in Him'* (1 Chronicles 5:20).

Concerning Gad's brother, Jacob announced:

> 'Bread from Asher shall be rich,
> And he shall yield royal dainties.' (Genesis 49:20)

One would not expect the son of a maid to be associated with royal dainties except, perhaps, to serve. Yet, Asher was to be master of them. Jacob shows, once again, that we cannot predict success according to parentage; God will bless whom He will bless, for there is no partiality with the Lord. Moses added to this prophecy, declaring:

> '... *Asher is most blessed of sons;*
> *Let him be favored by his brothers,*
> *And let him dip his foot in oil.'* (Deuteronomy 33:24)

The land that Asher inherited bordered with Carmel, on the Great Sea (Joshua 19:24–31), and was a land full of rich soil and minerals. Asher, then, not only had sufficient to provide for their tribal needs, but were also able to export their riches to neighbouring Israelites; for the sharing of royal dainties a brother will always be highly favoured!

Jacob related to the character of Bilhah's second son:

> 'Naphtali is a hind let loose: he giveth godly words.'
> (Genesis 49:21, AV)

As the two members in the sentence have no connection, this verse causes contention between scholars. Boothroyd suggests a more correct translation comes in changing the pronunciation of the Hebrew words. In the New English Bible (1970), we read, *'Naphtali is a spreading terebinth putting forth lovely boughs.'* This prophecy would then direct us to Naphtali's inheritance, a fertile land, itself containing terebinth trees, which they were able to make fruitful (Joshua 19:32–39). If, however, we choose to remain with the Authorised Version, we would look rather to the character of Naphtali and his descendants. We know that Jacob loved Joseph more than he loved his other sons, but perhaps a quality he appreciated in Naphtali was his ability to encourage others with godly words. As a prophecy for the tribe of Naphtali, Jacob's words did not signify a brave troop ready for war, but instead one who would succeed as they sought peace through godly words. Barak was of the tribe of Naphtali. In the beginning, when he sought the blessing of God via Deborah the judge, he was timid and fearful, unwilling to go to battle without Deborah, although he was successful in the end (Jude 4:8–22).

Jacob, perhaps leaving the best till last, finally spoke of his two favourite sons, Joseph and Benjamin. Jacob described Joseph as *'a fruitful bough'* whose *'branches run over the wall'* (Genesis 49:22). Whereas Jacob spoke plainly about the sins of his sons Reuben, Simeon, and Levi, here he spoke analogically of Joseph's life:

> *'The archers have bitterly grieved him,*
> *Shot at him and hated him.'* (Genesis 49:23)

In this short verse, Jacob covered many years of Joseph's life, from the abuse that he suffered at the hands of his brothers, to his time in prison. Speaking indirectly of the blows that Joseph suffered, Jacob showed empathy towards him for the pain he had suffered without alienating his other sons; as Joseph had forgiven his brothers for selling him into slavery (Genesis 45:8), it would be both unnecessary and unwise for Jacob to reopen resolved contentions.

Jacob continued the historical monologue:

> *'But his bow remained in strength,*
> *And the arms of his hands were made strong*
> *By the hands of the Mighty God of Jacob.'* (Genesis 49:24)

What has already happened in Joseph's life was linked to the blessings of God upon his posterity, and so Jacob promised:

> *'By the God of your father who will help you,*
> *And by the Almighty who will bless you*
> *With blessings of heaven above,*
> *Blessings of the deep that lies beneath,*
> *Blessings of the breasts and of the womb.'* (Genesis 49:25)

Joseph was indeed to be blessed greatly, for as Jacob realised that he has been blessed greater than his ancestors, he declared:

> *'They shall be on the head of Joseph,*
> *And on the crown of the head of him who was separate from his brothers.'* (Genesis 49:26b)

Joseph was physically separated from his brothers for a time, but the separation that brought rich reward was his separation in honouring God in every situation; never did he sinfully respond to the circumstances that he found himself in. Joshua, a descendant of Joseph, also separated himself to God, and so was chosen by the Lord to lead the people into the Promised Land (Joshua 1:2).

Joseph's descendants were richly blessed because of his devotion to the Lord. A double portion was to go to Joseph's posterity through the tribes of his sons, Ephraim and Manasseh. With great joy, as Joseph brought his sons near to Jacob, his father responded, *'I had not thought to see your face; but in fact, God has also shown me your offspring!'* (Genesis 48:11). Before dying, Jacob claimed Joseph's sons as his own; as sons of an Egyptian woman, brought up in the land of Egypt and surrounded by their customs and beliefs, they needed to receive their inheritance in the Promised Land in a striking way. The sons of Joseph, then, became equal with Jacob's own sons, each receiving a portion of the Promised Land.

Moses reiterated the blessing of the Lord upon the posterity of Joseph:

> *'With the precious things of the earth and its fullness ...*
> *Let the blessings come on the head of Joseph ...'*
> (Deuteronomy 33:16)

We see the fulfilment of this blessing in many ways; Ephraim, as having the blessing of the firstborn, inherited the finest and most fruitful land in the centre of the country, Mount Ephraim, with the Plain of Sharon to the west, Esdraelon to the north, and the Jordan valley to the east. A descendant of Manasseh, Zelophehad had no sons, only daughters, so the women claimed the inheritance promised to their family line, receiving the abundant blessings promised to Joseph (Joshua 17:3–4). As God promised them, how could man refuse them? When the tribes of Ephraim and Manasseh asked for even more land they were not refused but given the mountain area that towered over the Promised Land because they were recognised as *'a great people'* with *'great power'* (Joshua 17:17).

Benjamin's blessing was very different from the blessing of his brother Joseph, as it was much shorter and less affectionate:

> *'Benjamin is a ravenous wolf;*
> *In the morning he shall devour the prey,*
> *And at night he shall divide the spoil.'* (Genesis 49:27)

Perhaps Benjamin received his father's favour for over twenty years because he was the son of his beloved wife, Rachel, and brother of his slain son, Joseph, rather than on the merits of his own character. Jacob, united again with Joseph, may have realised his mistake – not that he would have stopped loving his youngest son, but that he may have taken Benjamin off the pedestal.

The prophecy that Jacob spoke over Benjamin described the Benjamites very well, as a tribe who went to war with the courage and ferocity of ravenous wolves. Descendants of Benjamin included King Saul, his son Jonathan, and Paul the Apostle, all of whom fought their battles with vigour and determination, 'devouring the prey'. And all were to 'divide the spoil'. Saul did so reluctantly, but eventually, David, of the tribe of Judah, received kingship. If we continue this analogy into the life of Paul the Apostle, then we can see that he shared in the blessings of a relationship with, and service to, the Lion of Judah, Jesus our King.

Jesus, our Lord, said that the meaning of eternal life is to become acquainted with, and know, the Father and Jesus whom He also sent (John 17:3). The meaning of mortal life, then, must be to develop relationships upon the earth. We cannot escape the fact that Jacob favoured his two youngest sons because they were children of his sweetheart. However, we are still able to observe that Jacob was able to appreciate godly qualities in some of his other sons, too.

Personal application

Jacob was a type of Father God in his role as father to his twelve sons. In blessing sons who had sinned against him, Jacob represents the Father God who willingly fathers all people and all nations, being *'kind to the unthankful and evil'* (Luke 6:35). Jacob's children received punishment for their sin. God also has a special father–child relationship with believers, protecting and admonishing when necessary, *'For whom the* Lord *loves, He chastens'* (Hebrews 12:6). As Jacob loved Joseph more than he loved his other children, so Father God has a unique relationship with Jesus, of whom He says, *'This is My beloved Son. Hear Him!'* (Mark 9:7).

A part of our Christian calling is to be in relationship with God our Father. Attributes of the Father-heart of God are woven throughout all the books of the New Testament (except John's third letter).

▶ Reading and meditating on the New Testament will bring us to a better understanding of God's Father-heart, and the relationship that He invites us into. To understand the context of any passage it is best to read it within the book or letter written, so choose to regularly read the New Testament from beginning to end. Pray for God to direct your daily reading. The amount read, whether two verses or two chapters, is not as important as feeding on God's Word regularly.

Chapter 16

Love Conquers All: Joseph and the Lord

Joseph's life, like his grandfather Isaac before him, marked him as a type of Christ. Joseph, being born to a barren mother, opened her womb for a second son to follow. Jesus, our Lord, born to a virgin, *'is the firstborn over all creation'* (Colossians 1:15), through whom we are adopted to become sons of God (Galatians 3:26). We first begin to hear of Joseph as an individual when he was seventeen, establishing that he was loved by his father (Genesis 37:3). Although Jacob's love for Joseph appeared to have an unhealthy effect on relationships with Joseph's older brothers, perhaps, due to the difficult calling that Joseph had on his life, he needed to know his father's love in such a demonstrative way. Jesus also needed to know the love of the Father to remain committed throughout many trials and tribulations, concluding in death on the cross – and so the Father spoke audibly from heaven, *'You are My beloved Son, in whom I am well pleased'* (Mark 1:11).

God revealed truths to Joseph in dreams, showing him that his own family would bow down before him. It would take time for Joseph to comprehend the true meaning of the Lord's revelation for we gain understanding of God's plans through our life experiences. So too, our Lord Jesus began to understand that He had to die for our sins, yet that He would also rise again, and to Him every knee will bow and every tongue confess that He is Lord (Mark 8:31; Philippians 2:10–11). The Lord's revelation to Joseph, like the love of his father, would strengthen him in the many trials he was to experience.

In relationship with his brothers, Joseph continued to be a type for Christ. Joseph's brothers hated him (Genesis 37:4); Jesus acknowledged the animosity of the scribes and Pharisees as a fulfilment of Scripture, *'They hated Me without a cause'* (John 15:25; Psalm 69:4). The reasons for hate and the subsequent persecution towards Jesus and Joseph were the same – their brethren were unable to accept their claims of superiority. In Joseph's case, his brothers' hatred grew for him as he shared dreams of their bowing to him (Genesis 37:5). And yet, because of his dreams they envied him, which suggests that they perceived truth in Joseph's words (Genesis 37:11). In Jesus' case, both His teaching and performance of miracles caused people to hate and despise Him (John 15:24), culminating in the establishment plotting to have Him killed (Luke 20:19–20).

Jesus warns us that as followers of Christ we, too, will suffer persecution and hatred. Rejection and persecution carry pain, yet Jesus encourages:

> *'... when He, the Spirit of truth, has come, He will guide you into all truth ... He will tell you things to come.'* (John 16:13)

Stephen, a disciple of Jesus, whilst being stoned to death was, by the grace of God, able to see Jesus standing at the right hand of the Father, and prayed *'Lord, do not charge them with this sin'* (Acts 7:60). Our lives can also be transformed to a higher level, caring more for God's glory than we care for our own lives – indeed not loving our own lives, even unto death (John 15:21; Revelation 12:11).

While Joseph's brothers tended the sheep, Jacob sent Joseph to check all was well. As Joseph approached his brothers, *'even before he came near, they conspired against him to kill him'* (Genesis 37:18). Similarly, the chief priests and the elders of the people *'plotted to take Jesus by trickery and kill Him'* (Matthew 26:4). Joseph's brothers stripped him of his tunic of many colours because it caused them great offence as it embellished him with the privileges and birthright of the firstborn son (Genesis 37:23). Jesus, because His teachings offended the Jewish authorities, especially when He spoke of being the Son of God, and was therefore sentenced to death. Joseph, in his ordeal, was cast into a pit (Genesis 37:24). His brothers, in conversation more than two decades later, revealed to us that Joseph was emotionally, as well as physically, thrust into a pit; *'we saw the anguish of his soul when he pleaded with us, and we would not hear'* (Genesis 42:21). Jesus was *'counted with those who go down to the pit'* (Psalm 88:4), carrying our every sin and sickness, fear and anxiety upon the cross. Joseph was disturbed by his brothers' violent treatment against him, and Jesus knew the physical, mental, emotional and spiritual torture that He was to suffer for our sakes:

> *'And being in agony ... His sweat became like great drops of blood falling down to the ground.'* (Luke 22:44)

We should, therefore, not expect from ourselves a super-spiritual response when we suffer wrong, but rather be 'real' – expressing our anguish usually precedes forgiveness and healing.

With Joseph in the pit, and food in the pot, his brothers sat down to eat when Judah, spying a group of Ishmaelites travelling towards Egypt, suggested, *'Come, and let us sell him'* (Genesis 37:27). The brothers sold Joseph for twenty shekels of silver to become a slave in Egypt (Genesis 37:28). In comparison, Judas also sold Jesus to the chief priests for thirty pieces of silver, the compensation price for a servant killed by an ox! (Exodus 21:32). For Joseph the betrayal of his brothers was a shock, yet Jesus, knowing all things, said,

> *'The Son of Man indeed goes just as it is written of Him, but woe to that man by whom the Son of Man is betrayed!'*
> (Mark 14:21)

We best begin to see Joseph's strength of character when we read of his life in Egypt. Sold to Potiphar, an officer of Pharaoh, Joseph rose to become overseer of his house. Even as a slave, Joseph was seen as *'a successful man'* (Genesis 39:2), the Lord being with him. What a lesson for 21st-century Christians! The Bible does not shamefully skim over the years that Joseph was a slave, but declares that he was successful because the Lord was with him. The world attaches little value to menial jobs, yet our Lord moulds us through the experience, if we allow Him. Look again at Stephen; chosen to serve tables, he became the first Christian martyr (Acts 6:2, 5; 7:59). Are there people in the body of Christ, too proud to enter their calling through the workman's entrance, and therefore left unequipped for their special calling? There's a world of difference in man's perception of 'humiliating' jobs and God's intention of using the experience to create in us *'a clean heart'* (Psalm 51:10). The former description conjures up images of toil without recognition, but the latter a wealth of reward.

'Joseph was handsome in form and appearance' (Genesis 39:6b). Potiphar's wife lusted after this young man, and asked him to lie with her. Joseph, honouring both his master and His Lord God, refused saying,

> *'There is no one greater in this house than I, nor has he* [my master] *kept back anything from me but you, because you are his wife. How then can I do this great wickedness, and sin against God?'* (Genesis 39:9)

Had Joseph been hungry for success, he could have thought it best to keep the mistress of the house sweet, but by living by the Word of God, he knew that God's favour alone prospered him. Finding herself alone in the house with Joseph, Potiphar's wife made a pass at him, but Joseph ran from her presence, leaving his garment behind. Unable to fulfil her lust, Potiphar's wife became revengeful, and accused Joseph of attempting to seduce her (Genesis 39:17–18). Potiphar, in anger, had Joseph imprisoned. So too in comparison, the chief priests found false witnesses in order to execute Jesus, of whom they had become increasingly jealous (Matthew 26:59–60).

Prison life was a new chapter in Joseph's biography, and lasted at least two years (Genesis 41:1). A slave accused of the attempted rape of an Egyptian would normally have been killed. Whatever reasoning was in Potiphar's heart and mind, the Lord willed that Joseph would be imprisoned rather than slain. Joseph was sent to a harsh prison, used mainly to incarcerate people who had offended the Pharaoh, which is not to be confused with prison of today's western standards. Joseph suffered physically for *'They hurt his feet with fetters, he was laid in irons'* (Psalm 105:18). Jesus was also unjustly bound in order to be led away and delivered to Pontius Pilate (Matthew 27:2).

In prison, Joseph flourished, as he had done in service to Potiphar:

> *'. . . the L*ORD *was with Joseph and showed him mercy, and He gave Him favor in the sight of the keeper of the prison.'*
> (Genesis 39:21)

Joseph chose to be in close relationship with the Lord and so was able to recognise God's blessings. Jesus, when dying on the cross for our sins,

> '... cried out with a loud voice. He said "Father, into Your hands I commit My spirit" ... So when the centurion saw what had happened, he glorified God, saying, "Certainly this was a righteous Man!"'
> (Luke 23:46, 47)

The people around Jesus and Joseph could see the righteousness of God in their lives because of their gracious responses to the injustices brought against them. Joseph, suffering unjust imprisonment, did not continually protest his innocence. He responded like Jesus who *'was oppressed and afflicted, yet He opened not His mouth'* (Isaiah 53:7). Again, only relationship with the Lord can bring you to this place of humility and acceptance. If, in an unjust situation, the Lord's direction is for you not to defend yourself, then He will also give you the peace to accept His will:

> 'and the peace of God, which surpasses all understanding, will guard your hearts and minds through Christ Jesus.'
> (Philippians 4:7)

Without it you will not be able to stand the pressure of condemnation.

I was locked in a police cell two years ago, albeit only for a few hours. As I waited for a lawyer to arrive, I travelled through many emotions; I knew what I was being accused of, but couldn't work out what evidence had led the police to their absurd conclusion. One minute I rejoiced in my God rescuing me, and the next I wept at the confusion I felt. I prayed blessings over the police force and I came against the many demonic forces fighting for control in the building. I was reminded of the scripture that the Lord gave to me when I first came home:

> '... seek the peace of the city where I have caused you to be carried away captive, and pray to the LORD for it; for in its peace you will have peace.'
> (Jeremiah 29:7)

I never knew that my Lord's word to me was going to become quite so literal but certainly, since that time, I've been much more determined in following His command! When it was time for me to be questioned, I realised that the hours alone in the cell were part of God's plan; I was both calm and strong, and replied without offence to their offensive suggestions. I was a witness to the love and power of God, not because of my own ability, but because the Holy Spirit had ministered to me for five hours. Some weeks later, I was told, 'This is not an apology, but we made a mistake!' Apology, or not, I forgive them and pray blessing over their careers – may God have taught them that seeking justice is more important than closing a case.

During Joseph's imprisonment, Pharaoh, offended by the butler and the baker, confined them to prison, and Joseph was given charge over them (Genesis 40:1–4). One night, the butler and the baker both had a dream. The Lord not only gives dreams to His own people, but also purposefully directs the heathen. Scripture tells us:

> *'In a dream, in a vision of the night,*
> *When deep sleep falls upon men,*
> *While slumbering on their beds,*
> *Then He opens the ears of men,*
> *And seals their instruction.'* (Job 33:15–16)

When the butler and the baker awoke they realised the dreams were divine, but grew sad not knowing what the interpretation was. This reads like a theatre production directed by the Lord God Himself, 'enter Joseph centre stage'.

Joseph was quick to notice the men's sad countenance, and asked them for the reason. Joseph's compassionate concern was obviously a characteristic that God had used to bring him into favour with all who met him in Egypt. Their dilemma of having no interpreter of dreams was speedily answered by Joseph, *'Do not interpretations belong to God? Tell them to me, please'* (Genesis 40:8). We need to follow Joseph's example in giving to the Lord the glory that is due to His name (1 Chronicles 16:29). Joseph was able to tell the butler that he would be restored to his butlership in three days time, and the baker that he would be executed on the same day, the day of Pharaoh's birthday. Like John the Baptist, the baker was to suffer as part of the ruler's birthday celebrations. Rulers without the wisdom of God to direct them are a fickle people, whose favour is not to be relied upon.

Joseph asked the butler to show favour to him when he was released, but the butler forgot his promise. What emotional turmoil Joseph must have gone through in the following days – first expecting to be released, then hoping to be released, and finally realising that he was forgotten! Such disappointments usually bring us to a place of greater reliance upon God for, unfortunately, the truth is that man will often let us down. Likewise, Jesus also met two convicts, who were crucified with our Saviour, but in this case, Jesus was the one making the promise. One, blasphemed Jesus, and so died in his sins. The other requested, *'Lord, remember me when You come into Your kingdom.'* (Luke 23:42). Our Lord graciously answered *'Assuredly, I say to you, today you will be with Me in Paradise'* (Luke 23:43). The baker, for a time, forgot his promise to Joseph, but Jesus, who is faithful, keeps His promise to the repentant sinner.

Joseph waited another two years to be recompensed for his kindness. When Pharaoh had a dream, which no one could interpret, the butler remembered his fault, and told Pharaoh about Joseph interpreting his and the baker's dreams correctly. Joseph was hastily brought to Pharaoh, but not before shaving and changing his clothes. When Pharaoh repeated the butler's good report of him, Joseph replied, *'It is not in me; God will give Pharaoh an answer of peace'* (Genesis 41:16). When I speak words of wisdom, two reasons that I know that it is 'not in me' are:

1. I'm usually hearing the words for the first time myself.
2. When I speak for myself, I'm often inarticulate and unable to find even the most basic of words to express myself.

Joseph could so easily have become dumbstruck in awe and wonder of such grand surroundings, and of Pharaoh in his royal apparel. Or he could have attempted to use his 'special gift' in order to receive recognition, rather than to direct Pharaoh's attention to the true source of interpretation. The years in prison, though, had not marred Joseph's confidence or integrity, for he was as sure of God's presence in a dungeon as he had been when a young lad at home with his father.

Joseph was able to interpret Pharaoh's two dreams, with both meaning the same; that seven years of plenty would be followed by seven years of famine:

> *'And the dream was repeated to Pharaoh twice because the thing is established by God, and God will shortly bring it to pass.'*
> (Genesis 41:32)

Joseph not only confidently interpreted the dreams, but also advised Pharaoh on how to prepare for the seven years of famine:

> *'Now therefore, let Pharaoh select a discerning and wise man, and set him over the land of Egypt . . . let him appoint officers over the land, to collect one fifth of the produce of the land in the seven plentiful years . . . Then that food shall be as a reserve for the land for the seven years of famine.'* (Genesis 41:33–34, 36)

Joseph spoke, not to impress, but because God gave him the wisdom to discern and advise Pharaoh. Subsequently, because of his wisdom, Pharaoh recognised that the Spirit of God was in him (Genesis 41:38). And so, Pharaoh chose Joseph to have authority over the land of Egypt, becoming second in command after Pharaoh.

In retrospect, we realise that had Joseph been released soon after the butler's exoneration, he would not have been given the opportunity to rise to power in such a miraculous way. Having suffered disappointment when the butler was not faithful to his promise, the wait proved to be worthwhile. In light of this revelation, we may begin to understand our own periods of 'imprisonment' and choose to patiently wait a little longer, as Joseph did, allowing God to fulfil His plans to give us hope and a future (Jeremiah 29:11). Again, we see in Joseph a symbolism of the Christ, elevated to a place of glory after suffering. After His death and resurrection, Jesus declared,

> *'Ought not the Christ to have suffered these things and to enter into His glory?'* (Luke 24:26)

Pharaoh called Joseph by the name of 'Zaphnaph-Paaneah' meaning 'a revealer of secrets' (Genesis 41:45). Scripture tells us, *'There is a God in heaven who reveals secrets'* (Daniel 2:28), and Paul the Apostle prayed for the Christians at Ephesus (faithful followers of Jesus, expressing love to the brethren)

> *'that the God of our Lord Jesus Christ, the Father of glory, may give to you the spirit of wisdom and revelation in the knowledge of Him.'* (Ephesians 1:17)

God, who is the same yesterday, today and forever more, is willing to reveal His secrets to and through His people today, as we continue to have faith in Jesus and love for His followers. However, the greatest revelation that any of us can receive is an introduction to the Father through Jesus Christ, for

> 'No one has seen God at any time. The only begotten Son, who is in the bosom of the Father, He has declared Him.'
> (John 1:18)

Pharaoh also gave Joseph a wife, Asenath, a daughter of Poti-Pherah, priest of On (Genesis 41:45b). In the choosing of a priestly wife, Pharaoh was showing honour to Joseph. Had Joseph been at home with his father, it would have been considered dishonouring for the favoured son to take a Gentile bride, yet throughout the history of Israel, God has introduced Gentiles into the line of Abraham. So too, non-Jewish people are invited to become the bride of Christ:

> 'that the Gentiles should be follow heirs, of the same body, and partakers of His promise in Christ through the gospel.'
> (Ephesians 3:6)

Thank God! Asenath bore Joseph two sons whom Joseph named. The first he named 'Manasseh', saying, *'For God has made me forget all my toil and all my father's house'* (Genesis 41:51). Joseph, as the second most important official in Egypt, could have requested to visit his family, or even have transported them to Egypt, yet instead he made a break with the past, and declared that God had made him forget the toil that family relationships had caused him. By Joseph's conduct in other matters, this cannot be classed as a bitter rejection of his past, but as a faithful acceptance of God's designs on his present circumstances.

> 'And the name of the second he called Ephraim: "For God has caused me to be fruitful in the land of my affliction."'
> (Genesis 41:52)

Again, Joseph gave thanks to God for His kind mercy upon him, which had transformed his life from that of a slave to a high official of Egypt. For, *'With men this is impossible, but with God all things are possible'* (Matthew 19:26).

The famine that Joseph predicted did not only affect Egypt, but neighbouring countries too. On hearing that food was stored in Egypt, many nations travelled to buy supplies from Joseph, and amongst them were Joseph's brothers (Genesis 42:3). Joseph immediately recognised his brothers and began to treat them harshly, not to exact revenge, but to encourage a confession of conscience as they were reminded of their own callousness towards Joseph more than twenty years before; *'Therefore, behold, his blood is now required of us'* (Genesis 42:22). The Lord can also appear harsh towards His creation in order to bring us to a place of repentance. Job declared:

> *'For you write bitter things against me,*
> *And make me inherit the iniquities of my youth.'* (Job 13:26)

However, the psalmist encourages us:

> *'For His anger is but for a moment,*
> *His favor is for life.'* (Psalm 30:5a)

The Lord, in bringing Joseph's brothers to Egypt to stand before the young ruler, caused much emotional turmoil for Joseph, who during each encounter needed to find a private place to weep (Genesis 42:24; 43:30). If we refer back to the naming of his first son, Manasseh, whereupon Joseph declared that God had made him forget the pain of his past, we may suppose, in the light of this new response, that Joseph had previously been in denial of the inner pain that he continually endured. However, I believe he had spoken in truth. My own experience has been that in my early years as a Christian I received healing that enabled me to forget the pain of my past, only for the Lord to later bring it all to the surface again for me to receive a much deeper healing. Sometimes, as young Christians, we are not strong enough to deal with issues on a deep level, or we may not have the support network that is needed. Later, when the Lord brings us face-to-face with our past, it is not a sign that the problem will reoccur throughout our lives, or that we will never be fully healed. Rather, it is a sign of God's merciful character having freed us through 'forgetfulness' while we grew in maturity and strength, which now enables us to confront and release the pain of injustice once and for all. Jesus *'died to sin once for all'* (Romans 6:10), inviting us into His resurrection power, but as individuals, we are ready at different times to bring our pain and sorrows before Him to be nailed to the cross. The Master Physician knows when our spirits and souls are fully prepared for a major operation. We need, therefore, to trust the timing of our healing to the Lord, who knows us better than we know ourselves.

Joseph's spirit and emotions were especially connected with his father and younger brother Benjamin, two family members who had not abused him. Joseph needed to know how they were, but unsure that he could trust his brothers, he instead chose to test their claims of being honest men by holding one captive while the others returned home to collect Benjamin. He may have feared that the older brothers had also sold Benjamin into slavery. Although we are called to forgive those who sin against us, we are not called into an unquestioning trust of them. Wisdom and discernment teaches us whom we can trust.

Eventually, the brothers returned with Benjamin, the sight of whom made it impossible for Joseph to remain disguised. Joseph revealed his identity to his brothers, weeping before them. The forgiveness that Joseph felt in his heart towards his brothers came flooding out in words of comfort and encouragement, *'So now it was not you who sent me here, but God'* (Genesis 45:8). As Christians, we are called to forgive in order to receive forgiveness (Matthew 6:12). Embarking upon the road of forgiveness creates much fear within. Does this mean we'll become a 'soft touch', or a 'mat' to be walked over? However, be reminded that in forgiving others we are forgiven, and therefore we are set free, not only from repented sin but also from the self-torture of unforgiveness. Far from becoming more vulnerable by developing a merciful attitude, we grow into confident individuals, increasingly able to direct events in our lives, and to understand the emotional reactions that they may evoke.

Misunderstanding forgiveness may encourage us to cry out against God's mercy, perceiving it to be a cruel eradicator of His justice. This fear, however, is not founded in the Word of God for Moses tells us unequivocally:

> *'The* LORD *is longsuffering and abundant in mercy, forgiving iniquity and transgression; but He by no means clears the guilty...'* (Numbers 14:18)

Our part is to trust to God every wrong that we have suffered, leaving the responsibility of righteous judgment to Him. Quite often, though agreeing with the principles of forgiveness, we don't actually 'feel like forgiving'. My belief is that, in our human strength, we are only capable of will-choice forgiveness. As we declare our willingness to forgive (even though we don't feel like it), the Lord enters our spirits with the power of true forgiveness, enabling us to rejoice in pardon of the perpetrator. Such depths of forgiveness cannot be humanly possible; only by the Holy Spirit enveloping us in the love of God can we express such mercy.

Joseph sent the brothers home to collect their father and the rest of the family. What a reunion it must have been between father and son – between Jacob and Joseph! We are told that Joseph *'wept on his* [Jacob's] *neck a good while'* (Genesis 46:29). We don't often allow ourselves the complete expression of physical affection, and feeling inhibited we pull ourselves out of the 'huddle' to allow our tongue to take control. Yet, 'actions speak louder than words!' Joseph would not allow himself to be inhibited by his extended family and servants looking on, but was real before them, holding his father close and weeping upon him for as long as felt right. Such acts require a maturity of spirit; a confidence that even if misunderstood or judged by others, we have the Lord's approval and acceptance.

Joseph was able to enjoy the renewed relationship with his father for seventeen years in Egypt before Jacob, knowing it was time for him to depart from this world, called for his favourite son. Jacob described Joseph as *'a fruitful bough by a well'* (Genesis 49:22). A fruitful bough brings pleasure to one's eye and taste buds, as well as satisfying a hungry stomach, whilst the well close by promises to quench one's thirst. Joseph, through all his trials and tribulations, brought great consolation to others, satisfying many a hungry soul. He is the most pure type for Christ in the Old Testament, with no sin defiling his character.

Joseph lived one hundred and ten years, around ninety of which were spent in Egypt. He was blessed to not only see his grandchildren, but also great-grandchildren. To be so long in one place and see his family grow up there, one would think that Joseph would have settled, calling Egypt his home. However, on his deathbed, Joseph spoke to his brethren, reminding them, *'God will surely visit you, and bring you out of this land to the land of which He swore to Abraham, to Isaac and to Jacob'* (Genesis 50:24), making them take an oath, *'you shall carry up my bones from here'* (Genesis 50:25). At the point of death, as through his life, Joseph was an encourager, expressing faith in the promises of the Lord God. Two hundred years later, our Lord delivered the people of Israel from Egypt, and Joseph's body was *'buried at Shechem, in the plot of ground which Jacob had bought ... which had become an inheritance of the children of Joseph'* (Joshua 24:32). Because

Joseph, in life, had been faithful to the Lord, even in death he was able to pass on the inherited blessings to his posterity, such is the faithfulness of God to His servants.

Personal application

Joseph was treated unjustly by many people and over many years, but still managed to remain positive in the face of so much adversity. When we suffer injustice, how can we make sure we grow through the experience, rather than become bitter?

- Joseph was realistic, admitting that people did things against him with evil intentions (Genesis 50:20). We sometimes find it difficult to admit that people who should have protected us have instead abused or neglected us, yet without being in truth we are not able to have the wounds healed.

- Joseph did not focus on people's intention when they sinned against him. On admitting the injustice forced against us, we must choose to forgive so that their sin against us does not damage us further by become our focus in life.

- Two decades after the event, Joseph was able to claim that the Lord, not his brothers, had sent him to Egypt (Genesis 45:8). This understanding was by divine revelation. We don't know when he came to a place of peace about his brother's act of injustice against him. We need, therefore, to give ourselves time and space to receive God's healing, and to pray for His divine revelation into our spirits, so that we may know that,

    '... all things work together for good to those who love God, to those who are called according to His purpose.'
    (Romans 8:28)

Chapter 17
Love and Hate: Joseph and His Brothers

Joseph, Rachel's son, was Jacob's eleventh son, but was treated as his firstborn. He was given a coat of many colours, a garment reserved for the head of a household and his heir. Joseph's brothers hated him, and were jealous of their father's love for him (Genesis 37:4). As open favouritism was a 'normal' part of family life for Jacob whilst growing up, he too brought this element into parenting. Although we cannot class favouritism as a sin, the consequences can be as deadly as sin.

On one occasion, feeding the flock with four of his brothers, Joseph reported them to his father for something that he felt deserved correction (Genesis 37:2). Here the author purposefully tells us that Israel loved Joseph more than his other sons. Whether the men were guilty or not, because of Israel's love for Joseph, they would not have expected a fair hearing. Perhaps, before Joseph's birth, his brothers never felt particularly loved by their father. Yet, seeing someone else showered with the affection that you long for forces rejection 'in your face'. Being an issue that is not dealt with, it often results in cruel words and actions, for *'out of the abundance of the heart the mouth speaks'* (Matthew 12:34). So, Joseph's brothers *'could not speak peaceably to him'* (Genesis 37:4).

To make matters worse, Joseph shared with his brothers a dream in which they were all harvesting in the field:

> '... *my sheaf arose and also stood upright; and indeed your sheaves stood all around and bowed down to my sheaf.'*
>
> (Genesis 37:7)

Joseph's brothers, on interpreting the dream as Joseph reigning over them, were indignant towards him and, *'So they hated him even more'* (Genesis 37:8). In receiving this negative response was Joseph arrogant, naïve, or just so excited about God giving him dreams that he went on to share a second dream with his brothers and father?

> *'... this time, the sun, the moon, and the eleven stars bowed down to me.'* (Genesis 37:9)

Joseph, evidently expecting the family to bow down to him, was rebuked by his father, who said, *'Shall your mother and I and your brothers indeed come to bow down to the earth before you?'* (Genesis 37:10). Even though their father rebuked Joseph, his brothers still envied him. Perhaps they feared that Joseph, being treated as the firstborn son, would inherit the blessing of the firstborn and thus, rise up to reign over them.

When Israel sent Joseph to check on his brothers, who were shepherding the flock,

> *'... they said to one another, "Look, this dreamer is coming! Come therefore, let us now kill him and cast him into some pit; and we shall say, 'Some wild beast has devoured him.' We shall see what will become of his dreams!"'* (Genesis 37:19-20)

Observe the jealousy and bitterness that was eating up these men! Their thoughts and actions can never be justified, but perhaps we can understand the brothers' resentment that was building up to this godless reaction. Without their father expressing overt favouritism towards Joseph, the older brothers would have, in all probability, laughed at Joseph's 'silly little dreams'; yet with favouritism lavished upon Joseph there was a question in their minds regarding the possibility of these dreams becoming reality.

Of all Israel's sons, Reuben, the firstborn, had the greatest reason to resent Joseph who 'stole' his position from him, yet he, hoping to rescue Joseph from his brothers' evil plot, persuaded the group, *'Shed no blood, but cast him into this pit which is in the wilderness, and do not lay a hand on him'* (Genesis 37:22). A story can be so familiar to us that we don't consider the desperation that Joseph must have felt as his brothers jealously tore the tunic of many colours off his back that was given to him by their father, and threw him into an empty well (Genesis 37:23-24).

Joseph pleaded with his brothers with *'anguish of soul'*, but they would not listen (Genesis 42:21).

A company of Ishmaelites soon passed, and Judah saw a way of disposing of his brother without becoming responsible for his death; *'let us sell him to the Ishmaelites'* (Genesis 37:27). The brothers who were present agreed, selling Joseph for twenty shekels of silver. Evidently, Reuben was not present; perhaps he was tending the sheep. On returning to the pit he was so distraught to realise that Joseph had disappeared, that he tore his clothes, a custom that continues today in the Middle East as an expression of intense grief. Reuben exclaimed to his brothers, *'The lad is no more; and I, where shall I go?'* (Genesis 37:30), showing the responsibility that he felt for Joseph, regardless of family friction. The nine other brothers, in contrast, caring only to convince Israel of their innocence, killed a kid goat, and dipped Joseph's tunic in the blood. Israel, as they anticipated, concluded that a wild beast had devoured Joseph. For over twenty years they were to live a lie, never confessing to the cruel sin that they had committed against their own brother.

Unbeknown to the brothers, Joseph had not been sentenced to a life of slavery, but had instead risen in power in Egypt, becoming the second greatest authority in the land. Thus, when over two decades later, they stood before their brother, *'lord of the land'* (Genesis 42:30), and now in his late thirties, we could hardly expect them to have recognised him. Yet, Joseph was, of course, able to recognise them. He began to speak roughly towards them, not as repayment for their cruelty towards him, but rather because he *'remembered the dreams which he had dreamed about them'* (Genesis 42:9). No word or dream from God is without reason, and will always be fulfilled in its due season. The dreams remembered by Joseph would have been accompanied by revelation; Joseph began to understand that the Lord had allowed his brothers to be controlled by their hatred, selling Joseph into slavery, so that the Lord could fulfil His promise to always provide for the descendants of Abraham (Genesis 12:2; 45:8). Like Joseph, it may be a number of years before we understand the dreams that God gives us. One friend, seeing herself in a vision surrounded by African children, thought that she was to become a missionary teacher, but was instead called to rescue street-children, becoming their 'mother'.

Joseph spoke to his brothers, through an interpreter, and accused them of being spies. Their claims to be *'honest men'*

(Genesis 42:31) must have been like a dagger in Joseph's soul. How honest, Joseph must have wondered, had they been with their father about his disappearance! And where was Benjamin, his little brother, who was only a child when Joseph was sold into slavery? Could their jealousy have caused them to do the same with him? How could he be certain that they spoke the truth when they claimed Benjamin was at home with their father? Joseph chose to respond to their claims by testing them. After imprisoning them for three days he said,

> '... *Do this and live, for I fear God: If you are honest men, let one of your brothers be confined to your prison house; but you, go and carry grain for the famine of your houses. And bring your youngest brother to me; so your words will be verified, and you shall not die.*' (Genesis 42:18–20)

Joseph not only needed to allow his brothers to return home in order to provide for his family back home, but he also needed to make sure that the brothers would return with Benjamin. He chose to keep one brother captive as 'a bond.' He encouraged the brothers with the confession *'I fear God'*, implying that no harm would come to the brother left behind.

'If you are honest men' (Genesis 42:19) is a very significant utterance from Joseph. He knew that the brothers of long ago were not honest men. If Joseph was a bitter person, he would have refused to believe that his brothers could change, yet he allowed them to prove their honesty. I see the work of the Holy Spirit so much in this decision, for our broken hearts, desperately clinging to what dignity we feel we have left, cry out of rejection, 'they'll never change'. In response, the Spirit of God gently reveals to us that they've already changed – for God is always at work, even while we aren't looking!

Simeon was chosen to remain captive. Joseph *'took Simeon from them and bound him before their eyes'* (Genesis 42:24). The family, who had bound their own brother and sold him as a slave, had to now watch as one of them was bound. It was not so much a bitter call from Joseph of 'see how I felt!' but rather a merciful call from God of 'repent and be saved'. In response to Joseph's command, the brothers, unaware that 'the ruler' understood their every word, spoke of their evil act against Joseph and the retribution that they felt they were now receiving. The guilt of sin does not diminish with time – if anything it tends to gain momentum except we repent and receive the forgiveness of Jesus Christ, who washes us from our sins in His own blood (Revelation 1:5).

Joseph, on hearing his brothers discuss their sin against him, and recalling the anguish with which he pleaded, also remembered that painful day in which he was rejected by his brothers and stolen away from the father he loved. Often, we are able to cope with a situation as long as we are not made to think or speak about it. We separate our emotions from the memory in order to cope with traumas in our lives. However, when we are forced to face the memories we will probably react as Joseph did; *'he turned himself away from them and wept'* (Genesis 42:24). This was not the last time that Joseph was to weep over the relationship with his brothers, but instead, marked the beginning of healing into much pain and anguish over his past. Satan loves for us to be fearful of showing our emotions, keeping us imprisoned in our grief and sorrow, yet the Lord promises, *'Cry unto Me and I will hear and answer you'* (Psalm 91:15, paraphrase).

Nine brothers returned to their father with both grain and the money in their bags. When one of the brothers realised that his money had been returned to him, the group became fearful, *'saying to one another, "What is this God has done to us?"'* (Genesis 42:28). Joseph acted in kindness, yet this secret blessing came after the brothers had been imprisoned for three days, and had been forced to leave one brother behind. Their heads must have been spinning as they attempted to reason their misfortune. Perhaps their guilty consciences were only able to argue that this must be God's retribution for their sin against Joseph. For when we are lost in our sin, we often begin to see everything as retribution, as our guilty consciences are unable to believe that God would bless us except when we deserve His kindness towards us.

Sending his brothers home, Joseph may have hoped for a speedy return. His hope, however, was to be deferred. Initially, Jacob refused to send Benjamin with his brothers, but when the grain was all eaten up, he reluctantly allowed his youngest son to travel to Egypt (Genesis 43:1–14). On their return Joseph, spotting Benjamin with the group, instantly gave orders for them to be taken to his home and for a meal to be prepared, eager to have his brothers dine with him. The brothers would not know how to figure out this 'stranger'; the last meeting had resulted in them being accused of being spies, and now they were invited to dine with him. So, why the sudden change, they wondered, except that it was a trap to enslave them (Genesis 43:18)? The brothers immediately attempted to give back the money that they had found in their sacks, yet Joseph's servant assured them that he had received their payment.

When Joseph returned to his home to dine with his brothers they bowed before him, just as Joseph's dream had predicted years before. This was an emotionally charged moment – the brothers desperately afraid and hoping to appease the untrusting ruler with gifts from Israel, whilst Joseph was longing to relate freely with his father and younger brother once again. Joseph, having been not yet ready to reveal his identity to his brothers, asked what may have appeared to be nothing more than a polite question: *'Is your father well, the old man of whom you spoke? Is he still alive?'* (Genesis 43:27). Joseph must have experienced deep relief as the brothers revealed, *'Your servant our father is in good health'* (Genesis 43:28). Joseph continued to hope, therefore, that he and his father would be reunited.

Having ascertained that his father was still alive, Joseph's attention turned to his mother's other son. Looking at him, he asked, *'Is this your younger brother of whom you spoke to me?'* (Genesis 43:29); *'his heart yearned for his brother; so Joseph made haste and sought somewhere to weep'* (Genesis 43:30). Joseph's desire was to relate to Benjamin as a brother, throwing off the cloak of pretence, but the time was not yet complete. After washing his face, Joseph returned, and chose to restrain his emotions, giving the command for lunch to be served.

The brothers were seated according to age, from the firstborn to the youngest, *'and the men looked at astonishment at one another'* (Genesis 43:33). With children, one may be able to guess the order of birth, but not with grown men. For the brothers, this was yet another unfathomable occurrence added to a confusing and frightening experience. The men were all given a serving of food, but Benjamin was given five times as much (Genesis 43:34). Often, the desire to bless can lead us to go a little over the top, and perhaps, in this instance, that's what Joseph did. The men *'drank and were merry with him* [Joseph]*'*, so this unusual incident did not bring fear upon the brothers.

The following morning, Joseph's brothers left with bags of grain upon each of their horses, and probably felt great relief that the whole episode was over. Their joy, however, was to be short lived. Joseph ordered the steward of his house to plant his silver cup in Benjamin's sack, and to then follow the brothers to accuse them of taking it. The brothers, certain of their innocence, contended the accusation with great pride, *'With whomever of your servants it* [the cup] *is found, let him die, and we also will be my lord's slaves'* (Genesis 44:9). Joseph's servant was ordered to reply, *'he with whom it is found shall be my slave, and you shall be blameless'* (Genesis 44:10). Again, knowing their innocence, the brothers had nothing to lose and so opened their bags for them to be searched.

The investigation began with the bag of the eldest, continuing in order to the youngest. The brothers must have grown in confidence as each bag was diligently searched and proven empty. But, they were in for the most terrible shock as the servant reached down into Benjamin's sack and pulled out the ruler's treasured possession. Benjamin was accused of stealing the cup and therefore, would become the governor's slave. In anguish, the brothers tore their clothes, before loading their donkeys to return to Joseph. Once there, Judah made a passionate plea to the governor, asking that he take the place of Benjamin as slave, explaining that their father's life was bound up in the life of his youngest son; therefore without Benjamin returning, Jacob would surely have died. From the onset of the relationship with the governor of Egypt, the brothers had insisted that they were honest men, but Joseph could never be sure he could trust them. As Judah courageously stood before him, willing to give his life for his brother, Joseph was able to witness honesty and faithfulness in his brothers, characteristics that were lacking in the days of their youth.

Unable to restrain himself any longer, Joseph, weeping, revealed his identity to his brothers. They, as we can expect, were dumbstruck – who wouldn't be! Joseph began to explain, *'I am Joseph your brother, whom you sold into Egypt'* (Genesis 45:4). Joseph, aware of the guilt that the brothers had felt over their cruel actions towards him, assured them they should not be angry with themselves, declaring, *'God sent me before you to preserve a posterity for you in the earth ... So now it was not you who sent me here, but God* (Genesis 45:7–8). What gracious words, words that could only be uttered by the lips of a healed person! God had healed the wounds that Joseph's brothers had inflicted upon him, and explained to Joseph why He had allowed it to happen.

We all cry out against the cruelty we suffer, but we don't always receive an answer from God. If our cry is an accusation against God, blaming Him for our pain, then our ears have become closed to His voice. If, however, we cry out to God, with an open heart and mind, we will be able to see, and even rejoice, in God's plans. He does not arrange for evil to attack us yet, *'all things work together for good to those who love God, to those who are the called according to His purpose'* (Romans 8:28), and *'no weapon formed against you shall prosper'* (Isaiah 54:17). The lesson, not only for Joseph but in our own lives also, is a painful one, but as Joseph was able to reveal God's purpose to his brothers, and send for his father, Joseph's sorrow was turned to joy:

> 'Weeping may endure for a night,
> But joy comes in the morning.'   (Psalm 30:5b)

In Joseph's explanation of the Lord's plan, he not only revealed what the Lord had already accomplished in the past, but also confidently shared the Lord's plans for the future. The famine was yet to continue for five years, but Joseph invited his family to dwell in Egypt, promising to provide for them there. He then wept together with Benjamin, holding him closely, something he'd probably longed to do since setting eyes on his 'baby brother'. Yet, the other brothers were not excluded from his affection; they were also are kissed and wept over. There was a marked difference in Benjamin's response and that of his other brothers. While Benjamin wept and kissed Joseph back, the others did not respond in kind to Joseph's affection. We can assume they were in shock, and perhaps they were still covered in guilt, even though Joseph had forgiven them. The truth is we cannot accept the forgiveness of others except we forgive ourselves first; our own unforgiving acts as a barrier, as solid as steel or concrete, to our hearts.

The sad truth is that even seventeen years later when their father died, the brothers, unsure of Joseph's love and forgiveness towards them, believed that all Joseph had done for them was for the benefit of their father. The brothers discussed the matter, fearing *'Perhaps Joseph will hate us, and may actually repay us for all the evil which we did to him'* (Genesis 50:15). They chose to send a message to Joseph claiming that their father had commanded them to ask on behalf of Jacob, forgiveness for his sons. Jacob, being so close to Joseph, probably knew intimately his son's gracious heart towards his brothers and would not, therefore, have needed to make any such request. On hearing it, Joseph wept. How heartbreaking for Joseph. He had only meant good for his brothers and yet still they didn't recognise the love that he had for them.

Joseph probably needed comforting, but instead he reached out to his brothers to console them acknowledging, *'you meant evil against me, but God meant it for good . . . Now therefore, do not be afraid; I will provide for you and your little ones'* (Genesis 50:20–21). There are times in our lives when we feel angry or upset about others misjudging our hearts and intentions, but like Joseph, we may be called to look beyond our own pain to the heart-cry of the perpetrator. Joseph scolding his brothers for lying about their father's command, and for not appreciating all he had done for them may have temporarily relieved Joseph's pain, but it would not have resolved any issues. Joseph was living out the command *'comfort each other'* (1 Thessalonians 5:11). If we are only able to comfort one another when our relationship is problem free, then we have travelled only a short distance in understanding the words of Jesus to carry one another's burdens. Joseph did not consider his brother's rejection of him to be the priority, but was willing to speak peace and forgiveness to them once more. How wonderful it is that our Lord Jesus also continues to speak peace and forgiveness to a fallen world, waiting patiently for us to receive the truth in to our hearts – that all are forgiven and accepted by the Father.

We are not informed if, after seventeen years of living with Joseph, the brothers eventually received Joseph's words as truth, but the Lord is willing to be longsuffering towards us, for a lifetime if necessary, because His heart's desire is for each of us to be confirmed in His love. Jesus paid the price for our sins (and even for those minor mistakes that we get hung up about!) by dying on the cross. Having paid such a high price for our salvation, the Lord considers it worthwhile to put in the effort in persuading us that we are loved and accepted just as we are, warts and all!

Personal application

Joseph was deeply wounded by his brothers' act of betrayal, yet was able not only to speak forgiveness towards them, but also to express pardon in a practical way by providing for their needs in Egypt. How was Joseph able to respond to rejection with such profound selflessness? God created humanity with the purpose of being accepted, so unless acceptance from another source is greater than the rejection we experience, we will respond negatively. We may reject others to protect ourselves from further pain, reject ourselves ('it's my fault'), or live in fear of rejection. Joseph presumably knew the love and acceptance of the Father, and was able to draw from God's abundant love all the acceptance that he needed to protect him from responding negatively. Rejection is painful, however close you are to the Lord, but depending on His acceptance we can all, like Joseph, be healed of the pain of rejection and be grateful for what God brings out of it.

When I was a child, I experienced a 'freak' accident where I began to sink on the local green as if in quicksand. My father was unwilling to rescue me, not wanting to ruin his Sunday suit. Instead, my older brother raced out of the house with only his jeans on, and rescued me. For many years, I told that story, concluding, 'I cried all afternoon because my suede shoes were ruined!' I seriously believed that that's what my tears were about, but the Lord recently revealed to me that I was not crying over ruined shoes, but because of rejection from my father. Then, in the Spirit, Father God gave me the most wonderful experience, rescuing me from the miry clay with His mighty hand, and allowing me to fly like an eagle. I was so excited about the experience I had with Father God, that I not only accepted my father's rejection, but also rejoiced in it – had I not been rejected in the first place I would not have received such an awesome recompense from the Lord!

There are 'steps to healing' which can lift us out of the cycle of rejection into the haven of acceptance:

- ▶ Meditate on the truth – God accepts you as you are and His love for you is unconditional with no strings attached! Some 'acceptance' scriptures are Psalms 23; 139:14, Jeremiah 29:11; Luke 15:11–24; John 10:27–29; Romans 8:14–16; 1 Peter 2:9.

- ▶ Recognise your need for healing from rejection. The root cause of rejection may be obvious to you, or like my 'quicksand' experience, you may need to pray for the Holy Spirit to connect the deep pain and the memory of rejection.

- ▶ Choose to forgive those who have rejected you in order for you to receive healing from Jesus – when we forgive, we are forgiven (Mark 11:25–26).

▸ Make a conscious decision to knock rejection off the throne by allowing God's acceptance of you to take precedence over self-rejection/rejection from others. Let God's word have the last say, even when you don't feel like it, and eventually His adoration of you and His belief in you will saturate your spirit.

▸ Choose to accept others as they are, following God's second most important command, *'You shall love your neighbour as yourself'* (Matthew 22:39). According to the spiritual law of sowing and reaping, you will be accepted unconditionally according to how well you unconditionally accept others (Galatians 6:7).

Bibliography

Collins Gem English Thesaurus (third edition, reprint 2001).
Illustrated Guide to the Bible (reprint, *Reader's Digest*, 1993).
Smiths Bible Dictionary, revised (Holman Bible Publishers).
Boyd, Robert T., *World's Bible Handbook* (Harvest House, 1991).
Dunn, Roland, *Don't Just Stand There, Pray Something!: Discover the Incredible Power of Intercessory Prayer* (Zondervan, 2001).
Dye, Colin, *Knowing the Father* (Sovereign World, 1998).
Elgar, Fred, *God's Unbreakable Word To You* (Surrey: The Millmead Centre).
Gass, Bob and Debby, *The Word for Today* (United Christian Broadcasting, 2002).
Henry, Matthew and Scott, Thomas, *Commentary on the Holy Bible* (Thomas Nelson, Inc., 1979).
Wilkinson, Bruce and Kopp, David, *Experiencing Spiritual Breakthroughs* (Multnomah, 2002).

Helpful Addresses

Ellel Ministries is an international non-denominational organisation that provides a variety of courses ranging from one-day seminars to eight-month training schools in evangelism, healing, and deliverance. Their head-centre address is:

> Ellel Grange
> Ellel
> Lancaster LA2 0HN
> England
> *Tel*: +44 (0)1524 751651

Or visit their website containing courses offered in each of their centres at:

> www.ellelministries.org

Lydia Fellowship is an international group that calls women to prayer, arranging local meetings, and national conferences, as well as providing prayer-focused literature. The UK head-office address is:

> Lydia Fellowship
> 121 Davey Drive
> Brighton
> E. Sussex BN1 7BF
> UK

The Word for Today is a free devotional produced by UCB (United Christian Broadcasters Ltd). To obtain tri-monthly editions write to their head-office:

> UCB
> PO Box 255
> Stoke-on-Trent ST4 8YY
> England

If you have enjoyed this book and would like to help us to send a copy of it and many other titles to needy pastors in the **Third World**, please write for further information or send your gift to:

**Sovereign World Trust
PO Box 777, Tonbridge
Kent TN11 0ZS
United Kingdom**

or to the **'Sovereign World'** distributor in your country.

Visit our website at **www.sovereign-world.org** for a full range of Sovereign World books.